A Short Jew in the Body of a Tall W.A.S.P.

A Short Jew in the Body of a Tall W.A.S.P.
by Mark Okun

Copyright © Mark Okun 2013, 2024
First published by Dog Ear Publishing in 2013

ISBN: 978-0-913123-45-4

Published by Galileo Books

FREEGALILEO.COM

A SHORT JEW IN THE BODY OF A TALL W.A.S.P.

(A Gay Melodrama)

Mark Okun

GALILEO PRESS

Contents

2012 Watertown, NY	1
Fanny Bagelman	3
Hair Today, Gone Tomorrow	15
Love, Peace and Hair	40
Utopia	56
Nights at the Saint, Summers on Fire Island	80
Beautiful Disco Fag	97
Spiraling	114
The Bottom	135
Sylvia	152
Makeovers You'll Never Forget	173
A Short Jew in the Body of a Tall Wasp	180
Have Scissors, Will Travel	196
Epilogue	209

2012 WATERTOWN, NY

I'm at my sister Charlene's funeral. I didn't even know I wanted to go. It was a freak coincidence that I called my nephew Dan I hadn't heard from in a while. When his wife answered she sounded stressed. Char wasn't well. She had forgotten how to swallow. Patty said they told her she probably wouldn't last through the week. I told Patty to keep me posted. I hadn't even had much to do with her since she went into the nursing home. I never went to visit her. But she was the one who filled in all the blanks.

    I had to figure out what I was going to do once she died. "Shouldn't I go to the funeral?" I really didn't want to go. That night at 2am I turned to stare at John. He was breathing heavily into his C-Pak machine. I looked outside at the cold New York City skyline. I had missed my brother's and my mother's services. I was so caught up in my work schedule and own affairs I never found the time. I had to go to this funeral.

    The next day when Dan called and said she had died. I figured I would just go alone. Maybe drive, maybe fly, I didn't know. I decided to fly. I rented a car and hooked up with Kip at the airport. We drove to Watertown together. I wasn't sure what condition he would be in when I picked him up but he was okay. I was glad to have a friend next to me. My nephew David who used to be a priest now turned real estate agent greeted us at the door. He turned to the first arrivals and said "Look at him, isn't he the spitting image of Alice Rose. If ever there was any doubt that he is her son just look at him. Now I was glad I came. They sat me in the second row with the immediate family. Kip sat in the back. David grabbed my arm and pulled me toward the casket. I didn't know what to expect. I hadn't seen her in ten years. She looked surprisingly good. He eyes were closed. Her rosary beads clutched in her hands. She had awfully good coloring for a dead person. I said a quick goodbye in my mind. I was there for the living, not for the dead.

This was my day to be the son of Alice Rose and it felt good to have my family all around me. Some people reconnect with family and recall their childhood. I had no childhood to recall. I'd only met this family when I was forty-two.

FANNY BAGELMAN

I don't know when I first realized I was gay; straight people are always asking. What I want to know is when did they realize they were straight? Being gay is like being left handed. You can hit a child with a ruler to force him to write with his right hand, but he'll still be left-handed.

As a child of four or five, I liked snakes, boats, cars and building forts; but I also liked dolls and dressing up in my grandmother's clothes. Of course, my adoptive parents, Abe and Sylvia, were always discouraging the latter kind of behavior.

I spent a lot of time at my grandmother's home. She lived only a few blocks from us, and my mother would take me there when she needed someone to watch me. Fanny was my best friend. She was a dark haired, heavy-set woman who dressed in nice dark suits brightened with jeweled pins and brooches, and furs. I loved the way the backs of her arms shook like Jell-O and her several chins bounced when she walked. She loved me more than all her other grandchildren even though I was adopted.

I was never aware of how much I didn't look Jewish like my parents. My mother Sylvia never wore jewelry or wanted to call attention to herself. She was 4'11", and my father

Abe, 5'2". Both were heavyset and had the black hair, olive complexions and brown eyes common to Eastern European Jews. Even though I looked like a tall skinny tow-headed WASP, everyone in the neighborhood knew who my family was, so they considered me Jewish. Strong Avenue was all Catholic school kids. They had been taught at school that the Jews killed Christ. The local candy store was at the end of Strong Avenue. I had to walk three blocks out of my way to get there, because if I walked down Strong Avenue, I would have been pelted with rocks and bottles, the kids calling me a dirty Jew. I found this to be not so much traumatic as inconvenient.

I hated being Jewish at Christmas. Not for any religious reason, but I was jealous of my friends who had brightly lit homes and beautiful Christmas trees. One year, right after Christmas, our neighbors threw out a small tree early. When my parents weren't looking, I snuck it up to my bedroom and spent the whole day cutting and pasting and making decorations. My mother freaked when she walked into my room to find a five-foot, fully decorated tree. "Mark, we're Jewish!" she screamed.

By this time, my parents had already told me I was adopted. When I was four, I had seen a soap opera where someone was adopted. I asked my mother if I was adopted too. She said, "Yes."

She explained that I was chosen and that all the other children's parents just got stuck with whom they got. I pictured my parents going to the baby store and picking me out, then taking me home. I wondered where these baby stores were. I also couldn't help wondering why they didn't pick a baby who looked more like them.

The next day I told my classmates that I was adopted. I said, "I was chosen and your parents just got stuck with you." They didn't believe me, so I dragged them home and asked Mommy to set them straight.

"Tell them, Mommy. Tell them I was adopted."

"But what difference does it make?"

"Tell them. Just tell them!"

I fantasized that Helen, my uncle's white trash girlfriend was my real mother. She was tall and blonde like me and not married. She had the biggest boobs in Syracuse. I believe she had two other children whom she had given up for adoption. But I knew this couldn't be true because Sylvia would never have allowed me to be around her. I was always fantasizing who my real mother was. I'd look at women on the street who resembled me and wonder "Is she my real mother?" I wondered about Marilyn Monroe. I looked more like her.

We spent summers on Lake Cazenovia, a small town about thirty miles east of Syracuse. My father and his brother, Uncle Phil, owned a four-bedroom cottage on the lake. My father had seven brothers and three sisters, so there were always some relatives visiting. When they bought the cottage in 1948, the area was "restricted." As you pulled into town, there was a restaurant sign that read "No Jews or Dogs Allowed." When my father bought the place, he'd sent Phil to close the deal. Phil was taller and blonde, so they thought Okun was an Irish name, O'Kun.

As we left the city of Syracuse and drove the country roads on our way to the cottage I would be excited about spending time with my summer friend, Joey. He was Italian and also adopted—a spoiled, only child, like me. Joey had dark skin and dark eyes, and he seemed exotic to me. In the summer, his skin turned a beautiful dark tan. I thought about his parents going out and picking him, like my parents did me. I could see why they chose Joey. He looked like them. His parents lived in one of the ten cottages on Overlook Tract, as did my family, but his family's cottage was a lot more luxurious than ours. Most of the other families in Cazenovia were wealthier than us.

Joey and I stayed busy with our lemonade stand. I also sold candy. My father had given me a five foot dinghy with a one horse power motor I had to wrap a string around and start like a lawnmower. I gave rides to kids who wanted to go to the swimming platform for a quarter a trip.

I was around eight or nine when Joey and I began to experiment sexually. Most of the boys were doing some sort of experimentation—showing each other how big their dick was, or trying to piss farther than the next.

One day I was trying out something I heard about in school—that by sucking hard on my arm, it would make a purple mark. I thought it looked sort of like a vampire mark. So I told Joey and we started sucking on each other's arms and necks. It was not sexual. We were just playing. We were pretending to be vampires and we did put a few marks on each other's arms and necks by the time the day was through. I was on my parent's porch with all our cousins and uncles when Joey's father came walking down the path to our cottage.

"Mark, where are your parents!? I want to talk to them!"

I went to get my mom. My father wasn't there. My mother came out and the two of them went to the other side of the porch. They told me to go in the house. Joey's dad was very angry. He pointed his finger in my mom's face and his face became beet red with rage. I could only hear words here and there, but I knew by what little I did hear that Joey's dad was angry with me for the vampire marks. My mother said very little in response; she had her head down as Joey's father yelled at her. Joey's father stomped off the porch and down the path, back to their cottage.

"Mark, what were you and Joey doing together? Were you doing something to make those marks on your neck?"

"We were playing vampire, Mom. It was just a game."

"Well, Joey's father didn't think it was just playing. As a matter of fact, he doesn't want you 'playing' with Joey anymore." She really did not make a big deal of it but I was incredibly sad. Joey was my only friend on the lake. I knew there was something terribly shameful in what I had done.

MY GRANDMOTHER FANNY SPOKE IN her Yiddish accent about my family. One of twelve children, she came to New York through Ellis Island in 1900 at the age of sixteen to escape the Russian oppression. She arrived with her two cousins. She was already an apprentice dressmaker and was confident in her abilities, using her chutzpah to get what she wanted. When the guard gave her male cousin a hard time about his paperwork, Fanny flirted with the guard to divert his attention and was waved in. Fanny taught me that life is there for the taking. All you need is the balls and hard work to get what you want. And a little flirting.

"Mark, ven I vas young," she said, "I came from very far avay in Russia. It is a very poor place, Russia, not like America. I had manny brodders and sisters, tvelve in all, but eight of my sisters and brodders died only children. Is like dat in Russia ... cold, not enough to eat. Your brodder or sister, dey get sick and notting to make dem better. To be a Jew in Russia is a terrible ting. Ve had to hide vat ve believe.

My modder, she taught me to sew. Dis she said vould buy me freedom."

I hung on every word.

"Mark, ven I came to America, I ves very afraid. I vas so far avay and I only haf my two cousins to show me vere to go. Ve stay on de Lower East Side vit some odder cousins who took in family from Russia. At night dey vould padlock de icebox. I move to Syracuse vere my modder's cousin married a vealthy shoe store owner. She got me a job as a seamstress for fife dollars a veek. In Syracuse, trew de shul, I met Moses Salutsky, your grandfadder. Moses and I, ve vant to get married. De people I vork for, dey like me. Dey give me a raise to seven dollars veek.

"But Moses, he til makes fife dollars a veek. I tell Moses dat he has to get a raise so dat ve can get married. I go to Moses' boss. I tell him, 'If you do not give Moses a raise to seven dollars a veek, I vill not marry him.' Dey gave him de raise, and ve vere married. Tanks God."

Once she went to see the film *Hell's Angels on Wheels* starring Jack Nicholson. She thought it was going to be like the Haley Mills movie, *The Trouble With Angels*. After the movie, she came tearing up to our house in her 1961 blue Chevy Nova, marched through the door and said to me in her most serious voice, "Markie, vat ever you do, I don't vant you to become a Hell's Angel! You should see dose boys. Dey came from nice families and dey broke dere modder's heart!"

Even as I grew older, I never tired of listening to my grandmother's stories. My perception of my father's family and my other relatives was all through Fanny's eyes.

"Abe Okun, your fadder, vas from a large Russian family. Dey came to America around 1890. His parents, Ben and Rose Okun, arrived at Ellis Island vit von child Harry. Dey live in Brownsville, Brooklyn vere dey haf four more children before dey move to Syracuse. A carpenter by trade, Ben Okun built a tree family house for them. Rose, she had fife more children; de next to youngest was your fadder, Abe.

"Ven Abe vas only seven years old, his fadder became very sick and died of cancer, leaving Rose vit ten cindilach to raise. Dis vas de Depression, and de loss to Rose and her children vas terrible. Rose took in laundry and sewing, and rented out de odder floors of der house. Dere vas little time for love and de children suffered, especially Abe.

"Ven your fadder Abe vas 13 and it vas time for his Bar Mitzvah, Rose — she had no money to pay de Rabbi. She vas so embarrassed. De Rabbi, he vould not have turned Rose avay. But Rose, vit her pride, she never had him Bar Mitzvahed. For a Jew, dis is a shameful ting. Abe was so small for his age. Fully grown, he's only 5'2."

I thought Abe hated me, but my father told me that he didn't know how to show love because he never learned how in his family. Fannie said that he really did love me, but I didn't believe her.

Fanny told me Aunt Sarah remembered when she and Uncle Charlie were first married. Abe was going off to war. She, Charlie, Rose, and two other brothers took Abe to the train station to see him off. She looked around at all the other families hugging, kissing and crying to see their loved ones off. The Okuns stood emotionless, shook Abe's hand and said goodbye, never knowing if they would see him again. And Sarah wondered to herself what kind of family she married into.

"My Sylvia, your modder vas de youngest of my shildren. She vas small for her age. She vas plump and sickly. I vorried for her healt. She never grew any taller den 4'11". She seemed only to meet tall men. Sarah, she vas smart, but shy. Dis embarrassed her to be vit dem, she vould come only to deir vaist and people vould stare.

"I sent all my children to college, to university. Sarah studied to become a social vorker and after de var, she vorked to find homes for Jewish refugees, Holocaust survivors. She had a kind heart. She had a beautiful biblical name, Sarah. Dis she tought vas old fashion, so she change her name to Sylvia.

"Now, Sylvia, she met Abe. Abe adored her. I tink Sylvia, she felt safe vit Abe. Dey vere de only two people short enough for each odder. She knew he vould do anything for her. Me, I wanted better for my Sarah. She was educated. She had a good job. Abe Okun, he vas not an educated man. I vorried dat he could not provide for her.

"Ven she vas a young voman, she became sick vit the rheumatic fever. De doctors dey thought she must haf operation, so at only 25 she vas going to be childless. She vanted children so very badly. Trew her job she knew a lawyer, Arthur Goldberg. Dis lawyer, he told her he knew a woman who was pregnant dat could not care for de child.

"I remember ven Sylvia came to tell me she vanted to adopt you, Mark. Dis she knew vas a mitzvah. She had been given God's most precious gift, a chance not just to be a vife, but to be a modder. Tears of joy filled her eyes. It vas a happy day. Ven she brought you home, you vas an angel from God... my *shannala analach*."

WHEN I WAS A CHILD, we lived in a modest neighborhood on the outskirts of Syracuse University's main campus. It was an older home that my parents never really decorated. As a result, we had the same green rug, tacky easy chair, and linoleum in the kitchen that was there when Sylvia and Abe first moved in. My parents never got a stick of new furniture from the day they were married until my Bar Mitzvah. For that occasion, my father wood paneled the entire house, so the whole place looked like everyone else's den. Then they got all new furniture. Unfortunately, they didn't share my sense of style; for the same money, I could have made the place really fabulous with a fountain in the living room.

Many of the large, older homes in my neighborhood were converted to apartments for off-campus student living. I always got a kick out of students' and out-of-towners' reactions to the weather. Most had never lived in a place where it began snowing one day and stopped two or three days later. The town, which is close to Lake Ontario, is almost directly in the middle of the Snow Belt. My memories of growing up in Syracuse include lots of snow. I mean feet, not inches. The local people are very resilient. They are used to snow beginning to fall in September or October and continuing through April and even May. The town is well equipped to clear the snow and nothing stops because of the weather.

Syracuse University is a private institution, not a state school, so the tuition is very high. For that reason and because it's not that far from New York City, it attracts a large, wealthy, Long Island, Jewish student body. The "townies," got a kick out of watching each new incoming class arrive with their expensive luggage, chauffeurs, impeccable outfits, only to find out that once the winter weather set in, they were better off in old flannel and snow boots.

My best friend, Michael, lived across the street. He was a gawky, skinny kid with a crew cut. His ears stuck out way too far. Michael's parents were devout Catholics, but they were also alcoholics. His mother and father separated, but could not get a divorce because of their religion. I liked spending time at Michael's house because we could do whatever we wanted. Most of the time, I don't think his parents cared what he did. Michael's mother drank beer all night. Their back porch was filled with cases of empty beer bottles waiting to be returned for the deposit.

Michael's mother was an attractive woman but her heavy drinking took a toll on her looks. She had a nice figure and she flaunted it. She'd go out to water the lawn in a bikini top and scandalize the neighbors. Michael's father was rarely home. Michael told me he sometimes lived at the Salvation Army. I was afraid of his father, as was Michael. He came to my house one time to borrow money from my parents. He looked drunk and unshaven. Abe gave him twenty dollars just to get rid of him. They weren't thrilled about me spending so much time over there, but they felt sorry for Michael and they knew I needed a friend.

Michael's home was sparsely furnished, but it had an expensive color T.V. stereo console set. I liked watching T.V. there because our set was an old black and white. Michael and I fooled around sexually from age eight to twelve.

One night I went to his house to stay over night to watch my favorite show on T.V. The Twilight Zone that didn't start til 10pm. I wasn't allowed to stay up that late at my house. I threw my PJs and my toothbrush in a bag and crossed the street to his house. When I got their he was already in his pajamas. His mom was drunk on the couch with a big quart bottle of beer in front of her. We watched a great episode about time travel. After the episode was over and his mom was passed out on the couch. Michael led me into his bedroom. I told Michael "let me see your penis. I will lick yours if you lick mine." He said "sure" Michael told me to pretend I was the woman and lay down on his bed. He layed on top of me and rubbed and humped each other but we were too young to know what a blow job was or even how to cum. In his bedroom, he had a huge wooden cross with a brass Jesus. I stared at the figurine with nails through the wrists and blood running down. It scared the shit out of me. I couldn't sleep all night, being Jewish and never having seen anything like it.

Michael and I were walking in the woods one day when an older boy, Peter, and his friend, Paul, jumped us. We knew Peter but tried to stay away from him because he had a reputation for being sadistic. As I watched, he punched Michael hard and held a knife to Michael's neck, then forced Michael to give his friend a blowjob. Afterwards, he called us both sissies and told everyone that Michael had given Paul a blowjob in the woods.

I was afraid of Peter and I wondered why he left me alone. I think Peter knew that if he had done that to me, my parents would've had him arrested. But Michael would never tell his parents. By the age of thirty-six, his mother died of cirrhosis of the liver. With no mom, and a father who was a drunk, Michael was sent away to live with his relatives in the south. We were twelve years old.

After Michael left, Peter began to taunt me. He would call me a girl and a faggot, and would beat me up even though he was smaller than I was. I didn't like to fight. When I tried to punch him back, the other boys laughed at me. They told me I punched like a girl. I was tall, skinny and awkward.

One day when Peter had to stay late after school, I waited for him outside. No one else was around. When he came outside, I grabbed him by the neck and beat the shit out of him, punching and kicking him and beating his head against the wall. I may have punched him like a girl, but Peter never bothered me again.

HAIR TODAY, GONE TOMORROW

I started to notice students on campus with long hair, beads, and dirty, frayed, bell-bottom jeans, rather than preppy Ivy League clothes. Many students dropped out of school but remained in off campus student housing near my home. Marshall Street, the main commercial block for the university and the center of campus life, became a mini Haight-Ashbury. Hippies, mostly from affluent families, hung out on the streets and begged for spare change.

I was thirteen and just starting to become aware of this new world. I tried to grow my own hair long and shaggy like the older college kids, but my parents kept making me cut it. I wanted to be part of the revolution that was going on in America. I started hanging out with two kids a year older than I was. Jeffrey and Sam were professors' sons who had been raised in a more liberal atmosphere. Their parents allowed them to grow their hair long and protest the war. I was young and naïve and didn't really understand the anti-war movement, but I loved the whole scene and being part of the in crowd. I joined People for Freedom and Peace, a Quaker organization, and handed out leaflets against the

Vietnam War. Bell-bottoms and peace signs became a regular part of my wardrobe.

I was drawn to this world because I never fit in with the jocks or the straight crowd at school. With the hippie freaks, I could grow my hair long and wear beads and sandals. I was totally accepted. I didn't have to be macho.

Throughout my young life, I was instructed in the Jewish faith. I attended Hebrew school and was to become Bar Mitzvah. But what did it mean to become a man? I had girlfriends and got along with girls, but as I became more aware of my attraction to men, I thought that I might grow out of it if I could just get away from my overprotective parents, whom I now towered over by a foot.

I didn't want to go to Hebrew School anymore. I thought going to the temple was just a fashion show for hypocrites and capitalist pigs. But my parents had prepared me for this day my whole life and they would not allow me to back out. I barely made it through my Bar Mitzvah. They had to send me for private Hebrew lessons so that I could get through the reading of the Torah and the recitation of the Haftorah.

I refused to cut my hair for my Bar Mitzvah and I didn't even want to wear a suit. I looked so different—six feet tall, thin, blonde and blue-eyed, standing next to my dark haired, brown eyed, and five-foot tall parents. I stood at the bimah and chanted my Haftorah so fast my Hebrew teacher came and tapped me on the shoulder to tell me the choir couldn't keep up with me! I turned to my Hebrew teacher and said emphatically, "After this, I'll never have to see you or this place again!"

When a young man becomes a Bar Mitzvah, he's supposed to write and recite his own speech before the entire congregation. It is usually about what it means to become a man. I wrote a speech about how we as Jews had to join with our black brothers and sisters and compared the yoke of slavery to the evils of the Holocaust. The rabbi rewrote my speech and only allowed one line about supporting the civil rights movement.

I invited every hippie I knew to the Kiddish at the temple afterwards. I wanted to shock the members of the congregation. I wanted to be totally different than the establishment I came from. The Bar Mitzvah ceremony marks the occasion when a boy becomes a man. For me it was much more like becoming someone else. I wanted to enter this new world of love, peace and hair.

When my Bar Mitzvah was over, so was my willingness to conform. My parents began to worry about my behavior. I was not yet using drugs, but I had started hanging out with a group of nineteen to twenty-one year olds, some of whom had "love children." I looked older than my thirteen years.

We often would hang out at the "crash pad" of a hippie couple whose names were Ginny and Dave. There were black lights, posters all over the walls, beaded curtains and the ceilings were painted black with day glow designs. Incense burned from metal holders and mattresses were on the floor. Old, large, wooden, wire spools served as tables and were the only furniture. Two cats and a dog were there but seemed to belong to no one in particular.

One of the girls, a willowy brunette named Lila and I were sitting in the living room one day and Lila was smoking a cigarette. I asked her if I could bum one from her.

"Mark," she scolded, "You're too young. Don't you know cigarettes are bad for you? They'll stunt your growth—although in your case that might not be such a bad idea. If you want to smoke something, you should smoke this!"

"I don't know, Lila. I think I should wait until I'm at least sixteen, then at eighteen I should try LSD; otherwise I won't have anything to look forward to when I'm older," I answered.

"Nah—pot's not nearly as bad for you as cigarettes," she said, as she took out a small plastic bag and some rolling papers from her purse and rolled a joint.

She put the joint in my mouth and lit it, then showed me how to inhale deeply and keep the smoke in my lungs as long as I could; I followed her instructions, but nothing happened. I didn't feel a thing. Everyone kept laughing at something, but I didn't get the joke. I pretended to laugh along with them, but had no idea what was so funny.

I would go to pot parties at crash pads whenever I could. Sometimes the older hippies appeared nervous about my age, but they let me in anyway. I'd sit in a corner and smoke and listen to the beat of Sergeant Pepper's Lonely Hearts Club Band. By the seventh time I smoked pot I finally got the joke.

I had to lie to my parents in order to stay out late with all these hippie freaks who had their own apartments. I would say I was staying over to a friend's house. Sometimes my mother would call looking for me and I wouldn't be there. My parents and I began fighting all of the time, about almost everything. I felt I belonged to this new extended family my hippie world had become. I wasn't willing to compromise by being a part-time hippie. This was the first time in my life I was accepted and not regarded as an effeminate nerd, as I was in school.

My first adult sexual experiences were at thirteen. I used to go to meetings on the Syracuse University campus. I was the youngest member of Students for a Democratic Society. I wish I could say I was truly a believer in a more democratic society but I thought they were just really cool. I also felt that I wanted to explore my sexuality. By now, I had a strong feeling that I was homosexual, or at the very least, bi. The treasurer of the SDS chapter was a tall and skinny guy named Walter, with a short Afro. He was the only person I had ever known who was openly gay. Since I wanted to find out if I was gay or not, I figured I'd try it with him. It never occurred to me I had to be physically attracted to the person At thirteen, you can fuck a rock. I made it clear to Walter that I was interested.

Walter returned my advances, but it was a disaster. I realized as soon as he removed his wire-rimmed glasses that I wasn't at all attracted to him. I was truly grossed out when he tried to fuck me. I never even knew two guys could do that. This experience confused me. Now I thought I wasn't gay. I began to go out with girls I thought were hot. I lost my virginity for the second time to a girl, but I didn't find it any more satisfying.

For the first time in my life I felt accepted by a group of ultra hip people who were on the cutting edge of what was really happening and I felt important. Not all of it was lifestyle. I was also an artist and was brought into the Syracuse gifted young artist camp. They gave me my first show. I could decorate, paint, and draw whatever I wanted. I loved fashion illustrations. Men had only four fashion options: shorts, pants, shirts, shoes. But women had a hundred or so. For me, variety has always been the source of creativity and I looked for that in people too. After one especially late night, I walked into the house and my father went ballistic on me. Granted, it was 3:00 a.m.

"Mark, you are just thirteen years old and as long as you live in this house, you're going to live by our rules. You are not going to hang out with these pot head, long haired freaks and you're going to have to tell the truth about your whereabouts, or you'll not be permitted to leave the house on weekends."

This was how it was ever since I could remember. My parents were open-minded but over-protective. My mother was a social worker and had that liberal attitude that you need to work with the disadvantaged. But Abe was always yelling about picky little things. For being only 5'2", he was scary. In fact, I think it may have been a Napoleonic complex that caused him to fly into rages at the slightest thing.

By the time I reached thirteen and was nearly six feet tall, I wasn't afraid of him anymore. I just tuned him out; I tuned my mother out, too. I was unwilling to live by their rules and there was no turning back. Late one afternoon, a friend told me she had just copped some sunshine acid and she wanted to turn me on to half a tab. We popped the LSD and went to a friend's crash pad; so much for waiting till eighteen. When we got there, the friend introduced me to two guys, his friend Trip, who looked just like Jesus Christ, and his friend Space, who looked like a frog or a toad.

As the walls started to move, everything became iridescent. I loved the way it made me feel and I told my fellow trippers that I would do this more often if I didn't have to go home to my overly protective parents.

Trip was sympathetic. He said, "Wow, man … living in Syracuse with your parents must be a real drag. This place is nowhere. We just came from Loss An-ge-leez where it's always warm with plenty of Orange Sunshine to go around. L.A. is a really cool scene, man. You'd love hanging out on Sunset Strip, hangin' at Whiskey a Go Go. You run into Jim Morrison or Frank Zappa walking down the Strip or Jimi Hendrix shopping at Head East."

Space added, "There are lots of runaways in L.A.—a whole community of them. You know, if you ever want to do that, we'll give you a letter of introduction so you can stay with our friends, Sharon and Greg. They live in Echo Park where a lot of heads and freaks live now."

I planned my escape for a week. Abe worked at night so he was usually home during the day. My mother worked during the day. As the week progressed, my mother told me that on Thursday my father had to take my grandmother to the airport. Fanny was leaving for her month in Miami. I knew that on Wednesday, my father would be collecting rent from some apartments we owned and that he kept the money in a large metal file cabinet. I felt I was entitled to it because my parents always taught me that anything that was theirs was mine.

That money was my escape route, so I watched it carefully. Together with the cash, there were also several rolls of Indian Head pennies which he harvested from cigar jars full of pennies. He'd spend a night meticulously sorting them in hopes of finding a head dressed indigenous silhouette. I remembered Abe telling me that he was saving these to help pay for my college education. I felt really guilty about taking those coins and my guilt plagued me for years. When I was older, I started a rare coin collection of my own which I planned to give to Abe to replace what I'd taken.

On Thursday, because Abe was taking Fanny to the airport, I knew he would not have time to deposit the rent money in the bank before he left. I knew the house would be empty. Sylvia was at work and my dad was on his way to the airport. That morning I pretended to leave for school. When I saw that Abe had left my house, I snuck back in. I knew where he kept the file cabinet upstairs, but I didn't have a key to the house. We had a cellar door that was always kept locked and they kept sacks of potatoes against the cellar door. The night before, I unlocked the cellar door from the inside and replaced the sacks so they wouldn't notice anything. When the opportunity was right, I entered the house through the cellar door and headed for the filing cabinet where he kept the rent money. Inside there was more money than I'd ever seen in one place, six hundred dollars. I grabbed it quickly and stuffed it inside the pocket of my jeans. Then I carefully closed everything up.

I had never stolen anything in my life but I didn't consider this theft.

I took down my polka dot curtains, unscrewed my colored, light bulbs (my new crash pad would be groovy) and put all my clothes in an old overnight bag that I found in the cellar. I took my stereo, which in those days was a bulky yet lightweight piece of equipment that folded up and stuffed my socks and underwear inside the stereo speakers to save room.

I had bought a fake ID a while back for fifty dollars and used it all the time to get into bars. I had a Syracuse University I.D. and a New Jersey Driver's License that said I was nineteen years old. I had put my own picture over the other person's and covered it with another piece of laminate. Everything looked very real. I fit the description because I was six feet tall.

The house was eerily quiet. I felt apprehension and a real rush of exhilaration as I contemplated my freedom from the oppression of my parents and my boring Syracuse existence. I was bound for bigger things. In my mind, I had passed the point of no return and I could not look back.

I called a cab and left for the airport. As the cab rattled along, my mind drifted to LA, the Sunset Strip, freedom, crash pads, and hair. The snow was beginning to fall in nice even flakes, dusting the trees and roads with a white blanket. I got out of the cab and looked around. Goodbye to the frigid and judgmental northeast. No amount of pretty, white snow could disguise the cold reality of my unhappiness here.

I went up to the TWA desk and purchased a student half-fare ticket with my fake ID and the cash from my pocket. No one questioned me. I kept looking for signs of skepticism in the eyes of the TWA employees, but I guess they assumed I knew what I was doing. Of course, I did not. I had never even been on a plane before. The farthest away I'd ever been was Cleveland, to my cousin's wedding, on a bus with Sylvia. I checked my baggage and waited to board the plane.

As I sat in the waiting area, the reality of what I was doing began to set in. I was petrified. I had in my pocket the names and addresses of Space and Trip's friends and a note to them introducing me and saying I was cool and it was all right to let me stay there. I had no idea how I was going to find this place, or if it really even existed.

The loudspeaker announced the boarding of my flight to L.A. I got up and walked outside. In 1968 they had no jet-way; you had to walk out onto the runway to a flight of stairs to board the plane. I took my seat between two nuns. I was already feeling incredibly guilty for taking money from my parents and causing them to worry to death. I struck up a conversation with the older of the two sisters. I told her I was an artist and that I was going to L.A. to paint. There is nothing like looking at two nuns to bring out the guilt in a nice Jewish boy.

The plane stopped over in Chicago and passengers were permitted to exit the plane for the hour layover. I was so overwhelmed and afraid of getting lost that I just sat cemented to my seat. After an uneventful flight, the plane landed at LAX. A landscape of palm trees awaited my arrival. I had never seen a palm tree before that wasn't in a pot. I claimed my stereo and baggage at the baggage check and hailed a cab. Already, I missed my mom terribly. I couldn't believe I was doing this to her.

The cab driver was a middle-aged, Jewish looking guy who struck up a conversation with me. He asked where I was from and when I told him, he broke into a big smile.

"Syracuse—that's where I'm from. Small world."

As I said, "Yeah, small world," I thought. "Oh no, he's from Syracuse and he looks Jewish; He knows my parents!"

When he asked me what my name was, I told him the name on my fake I.D. I gave him the address listed on the paper given to me by Trip and Space. "Are you sure you want to go to there? That's a bad area," he said.

"Don't worry about me—I know what I am doing," I replied.

When we arrived, he helped me out of the cab; he looked concerned. "What type of instrument do you play?" he asked.

I looked at him, confused. "What do you mean?"

He pointed to my stereo. He thought it was some kind of instrument.

"Why don't you come home with me?" he offered, "Till you can find a better place to stay. My wife loves musicians." I must have really looked innocent. His kindness was making me feel guilty. I told him I'd be fine and he reluctantly left me there. I looked around. The neighborhood was bad, but

I thought it had atmosphere. At that age, I was too stupid to be afraid.

I strode up the walkway to the apartment and knocked on the door. No one was home, but the door was left unlocked. I opened the door and walked in. It was filthy and smelled like dirty cat litter. The ashtrays on the table were filled with cigarette butts and marijuana roaches. I was so exhausted, both physically and emotionally, that I really just wanted to find somewhere to go to sleep. I found an old mattress on the floor in one of the bedrooms. It had no sheet and only some old, worn, crumpled blankets heaped on top of it. I drifted off into a dead sleep, forgetting the enormity of what I'd done.

I woke to a scream. Standing over me was a young woman with long hair to her hip. She wore a white caftan and beads and bracelets, a pair of granny sunglasses and water buffalo sandals. There was also a skinny long-haired guy with her. "Who the hell are you and how did you get in here?" asked the guy.

I quickly answered, "The door was unlocked and, here, this is for you." I handed them the note of introduction from Trip and Space.

They read it and looked back at me; relieved I wasn't a murderer. Then they introduced themselves as Sharon and Greg. They told me it was a good thing I got there when I did, because they were moving the next day. Great, here I came three thousand miles all the way across the country, knowing no one, and now I was going to have nowhere to stay.

I must have appeared to be really pathetic because Sharon and Greg offered to let me come with them. I breathed a sigh relief. They asked me all about how I got there and where I was from. I didn't want to tell them the truth, because they might decide to call my parents. So, I made up a more exciting story to make them feel sorry for me.

"I came upstate from New York. My parents are very wealthy. They were always traveling to Europe and leaving me in the care of this old housekeeper who barely spoke English. If I didn't do what she said, she'd hit me with a belt. I tried to tell my parents what was happening, but they didn't care."

They listened attentively and seemed to believe me. There were a lot of runaways in L.A. In 1967, it seemed there was a revolution beginning to take hold. Sharon and Greg were originally from New Jersey.

Sharon waited tables in a coffee shop on the Strip. Greg didn't work. They told me when they got to L.A. they loved the freedom of it all, just hanging out, smoking weed, frequenting the coffee shops. They met a lot of great people from all over the country and they saw some great rock groups that played on the Strip.

They told me that at first the whole hippie thing was great, but after a while, their apartment seemed really dirty. They wanted to move to a nicer apartment, save money, move back to New Jersey and get married. First, Sharon had to give up the lesbian life on the side before Greg would marry her. I thought the apartment was just wonderful. Why anyone would want to move back to New Jersey and get married when they had a great crash pad in L.A. was beyond me.

Before I even had a chance to unpack, we all moved to a new apartment in the basement of an older couple's home. It was more of a middle class neighborhood and the place was clean. We couldn't bring the cats with us though.

Sharon and Greg became more like my parents. They didn't want me staying out late and they worried about the people I hung around with. They were afraid the cops would pick me up. Since they were older than I was, and I was only thirteen, they looked after me. They found me a job modeling for a lady artist, but I got fired after a week. I didn't really want to work anyway, but all my money had been spent. I started out with six hundred dollars. The plane ticket cost eighty dollars and I had to give Sharon and Greg two hundred dollars to help pay the rent and for food. It didn't take long to go through the rest.

When the New Jersey driver's license expired, the State of California just gave me a new driver's license. With the money from the antique coins, I bought Sharon and Greg an old 1949 Studebaker and I learned to drive it also.

Everything was going great but I was extremely home sick. One day Sharon and Greg came home and said in a serious tone, "Sit down, Mark, we need to talk to you?"

Sharon lit a cigarette and brushed the hair from her eyes. She looked sad and concerned. She said, "You know we told you we were planning to move to New Jersey to get married, right? Well, I guess we decided that now is the time. We really have gotten to love you."

I had been their son for a month.

Sharon looked like she was going to cry. I didn't know what was up. It seemed like something was really wrong. She continued, "We talked to some friends up the street and they said you can stay with them until you find a job and stuff, but you know you'll need to live and pay rent."

"Yeah, sure, Sharon, you both have been really good to me."

"Pack up all your things. Greg will call and get his friends to help move."

I knew something was up. It didn't feel right; both Sharon and Greg were acting strange. Sharon was crying and hugging me and saying how much she was going to miss me. When they left the apartment, I sat there, just kind of spacing out. There was a loud knock on the door. The landlady stood at the doorway with L.A.P.D. They told me it was time to go home.

The police were not very nice to me. They took me to an L.A. youth hall for the night, until they could put me on a plane the next day. When I opened my bags, I found a note:

> Dear Mark,
>
> We are sorry about the way we had to leave you, but we couldn't bear the thought of leaving you alone in L. A. to fend for yourself. You are so young and we were afraid something terrible would happen to you. We will always love you. Some day, you'll thank us for this.
>
> Love, Sharon and Greg

I really wasn't that upset. Actually, I was sort of relieved. I missed my mom terribly and I knew my parents must be worried sick about me. I couldn't even imagine how they were able to cope with not knowing where I was. It was four weeks since I left, and I had never told them or anyone where I was or even that I was safe. The police cut off all my hair, deloused me and put me in a cell in the youth hall. I watched as the police brought in all kinds of drugged out, scared looking kids. "Why are you here? One kid asked me. "For running away," I said. "You?" "I killed my cousin," he said. I had never been in a place like that before. I was a sheltered Jewish kid (but of course, I was doing my best to change that).

The police took me to the airport in handcuffs and put me on a plane for home. I felt so ashamed. It was the same flight—to Syracuse via Chicago. The flight was long and I had plenty of time to think about everything. I thought of my trip as an exhilarating life experience, but I also felt tremendous guilt at having caused my parents so much pain. Throughout my life—with all the dangerous, crazy and wild things I did—this was the one thing I truly regret and wish I could take back.

When the plane landed in Syracuse, Abe and Sylvia burst onto the runway. Sylvia's eyes were swollen and red. Even Abe, a man of little or no emotion, hugged me with all his might. I was crying too. If I ever doubted for a minute that my parents loved me, this doubt was gone forever. I loved them like never before. After I returned home, my parents decided that they were not strict enough. Their solution was to stop me from hanging around my older hippie friends. I had a 10:00 p.m. curfew on weekends and I was not allowed out on school nights. But I couldn't accept these new restrictions after all I had been through. I spent four weeks in L. A. living on my own, and now it seemed like I was a prisoner in my own home.

I ran away again three weeks later. This time I didn't even leave the state, because my parents locked up the cash. My girlfriend of the week, Carrie, and I hitchhiked the thirty miles to Cazenovia Lake. It was cold and dark when we broke into my Uncle Dave's summerhouse (down the lake from our cottage.) It was closed up for the winter, but I used my fake I.D. to jimmy the lock in the boathouse where the life preservers, tennis rackets and boating equipment were kept.

We were able to gain access to the main house through the boathouse. The electricity was off so we had to do something to get warm. We built a fire in the fireplace. I used the one match I had left to light a whole pile of newspapers in the fireplace, while Carrie scrambled looking around for firewood. We fell asleep in each other's arms on a bearskin rug in front of the fire.

In the morning it was freezing again. Carrie took the bearskin rug, wrapped it around herself, and we hitchhiked back to Syracuse. It's a wonder anyone picked us up. We must have been quite a sight, with the huge bear head hanging over Carrie's head, as we stood shivering on the side of the road.

We were walking down Marshall Street when Abe spotted us and he cornered me. He was red with rage, telling me our Cazenovia neighbors had called the police and told them they had spotted someone breaking into my uncle's house. I felt no remorse. In fact, I just yelled back at him, calling him a capitalist pig (which I called everyone over thirty at the time) while everyone in the street turned to stare. Abe, who was a foot shorter than me, dragged me back to the car and drove me home.

In the morning Abe and Sylvia took me to Family Court. No one spoke as we drove downtown to the courthouse. Sylvia cried as she told the judge that she loved me dearly, but could not control me. She told the judge that I kept running away and she was afraid something terrible would happen to me if something drastic wasn't done. My parents signed what was called a PINS petition. It meant you were an ungovernable minor. I never thought they would do this to me.

They brought me to the Hillbrook Detention Home on a cold Friday afternoon. The guards told me I had to mop the floors and clean the bathrooms. I told them I wasn't allowed to work on the Sabbath since I was Jewish, so they just gave me some clay to play with. I was the first Jewish kid ever to be sent to Hillbrook Detention Home.

I only stayed there for the weekend and was then sent home on two year's probation. My first probation officer was a real redneck and things were still extremely strained in our house. He soon retired though and Mrs. Roland took over. She was a beautiful French Canadian woman, young and really cool. She was kind to me and worked with my parents and recommended they compromise on issues like staying out late, clothes and hair. She convinced them to let me set up a space in the basement. Since it was unfinished, I used curtains to make fake walls and painted a checkerboard, black and white pattern on the floor. It was a way for me to leave home without leaving home.

I KNEW A GIRL NAMED Bridget when I was thirteen. She was a hippie and a few years older. She brought me to meet Mrs. Freeman, the mother of a black guy she once dated. The Freeman house was on South Cross Avenue in a neighborhood scattered with hippie pads and university housing and adjoined a black neighborhood. Mrs. Freeman's home had once been a Victorian mansion but over time had been divided into apartments. Hers was on the entire parlour floor. Bridget and I entered through two oak pocket doors that slid into the wall. Smokey Robinson was playing on the stereo console. Various people were dancing, everyone was drinking Ripple wine. I thought it was so cool. There were all kinds of people at Mrs. Freeman's—black people of every shade, white girls and hippies.

Mrs. Freeman was a light-skinned black woman who could have passed for Italian, but she really looked Puerto Rican. Puerto Ricans had not yet come so far North as

Syracuse yet. She had eight children, but two were not home at the time. She introduced me to her sons Eddy, Danny, and Kip, and her daughters Paulette, Patty, and Star whom I recognized from my junior highschool.

I'd soon learn that Kipper was gay and that he had just started his first jo as a hair dresser. He slept in the back bedroom with his white boyfriend Billie McGee. I'd never seen that before, that a parent would allow that. But I wasn't like anyone in my own community. At Mrs. Freeman's I learned to stop looking for my reflection in everyone else. I'd walk through the sliding oak doors and whoever was inside would say Hi. I seemed to belong there. No one questioned my presence in their space. Knowing the Freemans also made school less scary since everyone knew I was part of their circle. During the 1960s even black kids couldn't hang out with white kids because other black kids would beat them up. But the Freemans were tough, and stood up for their friends. Everyone knew I was part of their family so no one bothered me.

The youngest girl, Star, who went to my school was also gay. Her girlfriend was a bartender named Spike. Mrs. Freeman accepted all of this without question, and I wondered if all black families were like that. Of course began to want to be black too. It was just so boring being white and Jewish, but the Freemans loved me as I was. I was lonely and started going to the Freeman's house every day.

I was so moved by their love of me. I was a spoiled white kid and they were a poor black family. My parents only had me, and I felt I was just an only child. They had to love me, But Mrs. Freeman had eight kids. She took her time with me and I was humbled by the experience. They taught me so much: how to dance, how to list to music—especially the words and how to feel them. I'm talking about the meaning of soul.

When I was 21 Star—who was the same age as me—died of a heroine overdose. Sister Patty called me right away and I went over to mourn with the family. I stayed close to all the other siblings my whole life and I still talk with Kipper a few times a week. Only three siblings are left today. Their children are adults now whom I've known since they were born and we are still friendly. A few years ago they had a Freeman reunion lunch for me at Syracuse. Whenever I go to San Francisco I stay with Eddy's son, Wheeler, who is fifty and gay. When they found an old photo of Kipper's great great grandparents with Harriet Tubman and sent me a copy. I have now enjoyed sixty years of Freeman love. I can never repay them. I can only share what I learned to others who need to learn it.

MY PARENTS BEGAN TO HEAR stories from other parents whose kids were growing their hair long and running away. Once they realized that it was not happening to just them alone, but was something that was happening all over America, they loosened up and we began to settle into a somewhat peaceful coexistence. In fact, my parents even started giving advice to their other friends whose kids were acting out. The social worker in Sylvia took over.

I never really fit in at school because I was bad at sports and couldn't fight. At Hebrew school, however, it didn't matter. You were cool if your parents were rich, but mine weren't.

Hanging out with older kids who were between nineteen and twenty-one, it made my peers in school act in awe (of me.) I started going to rock concerts at the War Memorial

Auditorium. Even though I was only fourteen years old, I was tall, had shoulder length hair and looked a lot older than I was. I not only wanted to attend the concerts and see the rock legends play, but to meet them and hangout backstage. When a great band was supposed to play, I'd sneak away after school and take a bus or hitch downtown. I'd scope out the place, walking all around waiting for the roadies to arrive and begin setting up the equipment and lighting for the concert that evening. I told them I had no money but I could help them set the stage if they would give me a back stage pass. I'd get sandwiches and help carry the heavy equipment out onto the stage. The roadies were more than willing to let me do their heavy lifting.

I met Jimi Hendrix and Robert Plant. I kept Janis Joplin's empty Southern Comfort bottle that I had stolen for years as a keepsake. It was more precious to me than the Hope Diamond. I sold it for fifty dollars. All of my friends would come to the concert and I would stand conspicuously on the right side of the stage wings, waving to my friends on the left side of the audience. Then I'd maneuver my way to the other side, so everyone could see me on the other side of the audience. This elevated my status in my high school to new levels. Even when I was busy denouncing all worldly and capitalist values, my desire for status still prevailed.

One night, Led Zeppelin was playing at the War Memorial. I did my usual routine of leaving school early and going downtown to hang around and try to associate myself with the roadies. I never told any of my friends how I did it because I was afraid they would all do it and that would ruin it for me. I introduced myself to the guys and began to help out in my usual way. One of the guys who let me in was a hot, swarthy English guy named George. He was the stage manager for Bo Didley, who was opening up for Led Zeppelin that night. He seemed to like me. He offered me some pot and we smoked a joint together. He invited me to come to the party after the show. Before the concert, Jimmy Page needed some makeup to wear on stage, because they left his in the last town.

"Mark," he said, "I've forgotten my makeup."

I asked girls in the front row if they had any spare make up for Jimmy. I was pummeled in a mascara rainstorm. I was so caught up in the razzle-dazzle of it all. When I came back on stage, George, the English guy, called to me to come back and help him move some equipment. I then followed him up in the rafters. As Jimmy Page and Led Zeppelin belted out "I ain't jokin' woman; I've got to ramble," George came up behind me and rubbed my neck and shoulders asking me if I felt fatigued from all the heavy lifting. Before I knew what was happening, he pulled me behind a curtain and climbed up the rafters. We sixty-nined with three thousand people just a few feet away.

As we got up and brushed ourselves off, George said, "I'll see you later, man, at the party."

"Sure, man, I wouldn't miss it for anything."

After the concert, I was waiting for the best part of the evening, to talk and party with my rock and roll heroes. The roadies began to pack up and put things away and I noticed that everyone was pretty much ignoring me. I felt like I was invisible to George. Everyone scurried around me to get out of there quickly and away from the throngs of fans waiting outside. I offered my help but was quickly rebuffed. One roadie told me, "It's okay pal, you've done enough, but thanks and we'll catch you next time."

I looked around for George. He walked right by me with his arm around a tall, black haired girl I knew from my junior high. He got in the van and drove away leaving me standing there alone.

Syracuse's drug problem in 1969 was perceived by the police to be out of control. In reality, there was only a small portion of the population using drugs, but this was something very foreign and frightening to the powers that be. Even though Syracuse is a city, in many ways it is a small town. The cops knew everybody and made it their business to know what everyone was doing. With little regard to your Fourth, Fifth and Fourteenth Amendment rights, if you had long hair, your telephone was tapped. And, of course, since I had shoulder length hair and hung out with the hippie, druggie crowd, this included me.

The police, as part of a sting operation, had been investigating all the long hair types in the University area on suspicion of using and dealing drugs. They had wiretaps on everyone's phones. I'd been dealing a little pot in junior high, but certainly nothing big. I would buy a quarter pound, mix it with oregano and cut it up into nickels. I'd have one nickel bag for myself every weekend.

It was a typical February morning. The snow was at least a foot deep and the temperature was in the teens. Everyone in the house was sound asleep. At about 5:00 a.m., there was pounding on the front door. Six uniformed policemen and a plain clothed officer were at my front door.

I heard Abe, who had just gotten home from work, run up the stairs and yell, "It's the police; I think they're here for Mark."

Sylvia screamed "Well, they're not here for us!"

The officers were armed with an indictment for my arrest on two felony charges and a misdemeanor handed down from the Grand Jury. Sylvia came downstairs in her housecoat. With total disregard for my parents and our property, they searched the house. They ripped books off the shelves. They opened drawers and rifled through them, leaving a total mess. The pulled sheets and blankets off the bed, looked under mattresses. They found nothing but the psychedelic room in the basement which they surprisingly never searched. It was where I kept a little pot and a scale. I was relived they never went down there.

Abe and Sylvia were mortified. They couldn't believe the callousness that the police had displayed. Sylvia timidly tried to express her dismay to the officers.

"We feel sorry for you and your husband, Mrs. Okun, but not for your son. He and his hippie friends are what are ruining this country. We have an indictment for him handed down by the Grand Jury of the State of New York."

"But officers, he's only fourteen."

"He keeps company with some bad people, Mrs. Okun, and they're all dealing and using drugs.

"But look at my house, look what you've done to our house."

"Like I said, Mrs. Okun, we're sorry that you and your husband have such a bad kid."

I was watching the whole scene from the staircase balcony. I was trying to stay out of everyone's way and hoping they couldn't find my other stash in the basement. My heart was pounding. They handcuffed me and took me away in a police car. I searched my parents' faces for signs of how angry they were. What I sensed was that they had reserved most of their anger for the police, because of the way they had ripped apart their house. Somehow I knew that this time they weren't going to throw me to the lions. My parent's support carried me through. I stared in silence at the police and refused to answer them when they asked me where my friends got their drugs.

"Who are they? Where are they?"

I would never give up my friends. My parents went to the police station with me. While I was being booked my friend G.G. from up the street was brought in, also in handcuffs. Then, in came Jeffrey one of my mother's Jewish history students from Temple, whose father was very prominent there. They both chimed in "Hi, Mrs. Okun," when they saw my mom. I was released into my parents' custody. They arrested twenty-seven adults and three juveniles.

When the case finally came up for trial, it was something of a joke. My uncle, Charlie, was representing me. The evidence against me was so flimsy, that the judge threw out the case.

My probation officer, Mrs. Roland was great. She told the judge I was doing well and should be taken off probation. She said that my parents and I were really trying to work together to get me back on track. I felt so lucky to have parents who supported me and didn't take sides with the pigs.

LOVE, PEACE AND HAIR

Arrest did little to change my partying ways. Drugs were everywhere and everyone was doing them. I had lost interest in school and was flunking out. All I really wanted to do was hang around with my friends, get high, grow my hair, and listen to music—anything from Janis Joplin to The Temptations. I loved acid rock and acid folk and I loved soul.

Kids in my crowd were on a rainbow of acid, diet pills, pot, and doughnuts. Some would sit at the end of the hallway called "the trench" and smoke pot all day. Others hung out at Carrol's Burger Shop or rode around in their cars tripping on acid. Hardly anyone went to class. This was the time when integration began and black kids were bused into the segregated schools. I don't know why black children had to be bused to our school rather than we be bused to their school. Most of the new black students wanted to beat up the white kids. I already didn't like going to school, but now I was afraid to. My cousin Scotty, Uncle Dave's son who was the same age as me, was thrown down a flight of stairs and ended up in traction for three weeks. The principal got hit over the head with a chair in the cafeteria and was rushed to the hospital. I knew a girl named Ceclia who kept razor blades in her Afro. If she got into a fight and someone grabbed her by the hair, they'd get cut. When I sensed things were getting out of hand at school I would sneak home through backyards so my parents' friends wouldn't see me and tell them I wasn't at school.

One of the girls in our hippie crowd was named Ginny. She was a schoolteacher and was the only one with a steady job. I met Harry Myers through Ginny. Ginny had recently moved from Syracuse back to the Bronx and she was working for Mercury Records in Manhattan and was having a New Year's Eve party in her new apartment. She invited me, but since I was only fifteen, I had to ask my parents' permission. By now, I'd worn down their resolve; my parents allowed me to do things that most parents wouldn't. Like, they let me go to Woodstock. I convinced them it would be like the Newport Jazz Festival. I drove there in a caravan of three vans and a few cars with thirty of my friends. Of course some cops pulled us over in the Catskills. I had $150 in my pocket, money my parents had given me to buy school clothes in the city since Syracuse stores didn't carry my size. The cops took all of it in the shakedown. My parents freaked out when they saw the Woodstock news on TV. They would have liked knowing I had such a miserable time. It was muddy, and nearly impossible to find a bushn to pee behind that didn't have someone already fucking in it. Don't even ask me about the outhouses. I held it for three days.

On New Year's Eve 1969, I took the 3:00 pm bus from Syracuse to New York City. Ginny's apartment in the Bronx was a third floor walk-up in an older building on the Grand Concourse, a formerly Jewish enclave that now was mostly Hispanic. She explained how it was close to where she had grown up. Some of her new friends from New York City stopped by and we all talked and smoked pot into the wee hours. I slept on the couch in front of the TV amid the cigarette butts and potato chip wrappers and awoke to the sound of the late night buzz indicating that broadcasting had come to an end.

I opened my eyes. A good looking blonde boy and Ginny's girlfriend from Syracuse were asleep together on a couch across the room. I wondered what this Adonis creature was all about. The next morning over coffee, Harry kept staring at me. It made me very nervous. He told me he was a student at Syracuse University and played in a band there. He was a German major and had only one year left to graduate.

There was another couple who had moved to Greenwich Village from Syracuse recently and I wanted to visit them. I asked Harry if I could bum fifty cents to take the subway, but he offered to drive me instead. In his car, he kept looking over at me and asking about the type of music I liked. I told him I liked Motown, the Airplane and Joplin. He told me he had a new apartment in Syracuse and would love for me to come and see it when I got back home. When we arrived at my friends' apartment, I waved goodbye to Harry and forgot about him.

Weeks later, while hitchhiking on Marshall Street in Syracuse, a car pulled over that looked familiar. Someone in the driver's seat was waving me to come over. It was Harry. Even though I was already late for supper and I knew Sylvia would be mad I said 'okay' to his renewed invitation to see his new place. His apartment was much nicer than the crash pad dumps I was hanging out at. He came from a wealthy Boston family and had his own car and credit cards, too. I went to see him many times. We started tonguing each other. The smell of his arm pits were better than any cologne. As we maneuvered our bodies around we began to sixty-nine.

The thought of this older man's cock down my throat with the feeling of my cock in his mouth was incredible. After we came we were both still hard. He let me know he wanted to fuck me. As he entered me I never felt such pain. I had never been fucked before but after awhile it began to feel good. The thought who was doing it to me was the best part. Harry was fucking beautiful. He and I had sex, great sex. When we were together our bodies just seemed to fit perfectly. I wanted to explore every inch of his body. His cock was massive and beautifully shaped. When he looked in my eye I could almost cum. I never knew I could feel that way with anyone and I thought this must be what they call love. This is what all those songs were about.

Neither Harry nor I were brave enough at the time, however, to talk openly about our feelings for each other. I thought that it was okay to be bisexual, but not homosexual. Apparently, Harry felt the same way. I also had a girlfriend named Judy. She had long wavy, dark hair, parted down the middle, reaching to her waist. She looked something like Janis Joplin. She was sixteen, a year older than me. I introduced Harry to her friend who we called Russian Cathy and we began to double date. This way we could go places and do things together, with the girls. The girls had no idea what was going on between us. We were also having sex with them. Abe and Sylvia loved Harry. He was so much more sophisticated and intelligent than my other friends. Harry was my blonde surfer god, the big brother I never had. The smell of his sweat made me hard.

Our foursome was working out pretty well until one day when Russian Cathy found a handmade Valentine I'd given to Harry. Cathy showed Judy the card and she freaked out. "Mark, I just can't believe this. After all these months of spending time together, the four of us, and all the nights we slept together, Harry and you were fucking behind my back. I thought you loved me. Mark, I'll be willing to stand by you, but only if you get help."

"Judy, I like the way I am. If it's good enough for Jagger, its good enough for me."

Judy cried for days and refused to ever see me again. Harry broke up with Cathy, quit school with only a semester left, moved to the East Village and joined a band called Steam. He continued to come back regularly to visit me on weekends. When he came, he'd stay at my parents' house. Sometimes, I'd invite my friend Laura to stay over at the same time so that I was forced to stay in the same room with Harry. My parents didn't let boys and girls sleep in the same room. I would also visit Harry in the East Village on East Seventh Street and Avenue C where untouched buildings stood shoulder with rubble and ruins so that the whole neighborhood felt attacked in some way. There were junkies, and people on speed who dressed in a Shakespearean way, like a Renaissance Fair for the Dark Ages. Harry had a bathtub in his kitchen and the toilet was down at the end of the hall outside his apartment. I was afraid to go outside for fear of rats and if I had to get up during the night, I would just pee in the sink.

Harry seemed to think living like this was great. He thought poverty was romantic. His parents still gave him money but it went for drugs. Harry's band, Steam, was doing very well. They had a hit song, "Na, Na, Hey, Hey, Kiss Him Goodbye." He was soon going on tour. I really didn't like the dirt and I was afraid of the junkies, but I tried to hide my fears. Besides, my boyfriend was a rock star! How many fifteen-year-old boys could say that?

During the day we would hang around with all the other hippies on St. Mark's Place. One day, Harry struck up a conversation with a pretty black girl named Rose. She said she had a small part in the play "Hair." I thought she was a junkie. We all drank some wine, smoked some pot and went back to Harry's apartment. We sat around drinking until we passed out. Later that night when Harry thought I was asleep, he snuck out of our bed into the living room where Rose was asleep on the couch. I could hear Harry fucking her. I had never been so upset. Since Harry moved to New York, I didn't get to see him nearly as much as I wanted. This was my Easter vacation from school. How could he do this to me on the one weekend I'd come all the way from Syracuse to be with him? I waited for him to come sneaking back into the bedroom. I jumped up out of the bed; I spit on him and beat him with my fists. "You fucking asshole—you two faced asshole!" I screamed. I kicked and beat him as hard as I could. Harry just started crying and kissing me and held my arms down. He pinned me down and we fucked for two hours. When he fell asleep, I packed up all my things and quietly crept out of the door without waking him. I looked down at the naked Rose on the couch as I closed the door behind me. I took a cab to Grand Central Station and bought a ticket to Boston. Harry and I had planned to go to Boston to visit some friends and see his parents. I decided to just go up and stay with my friends anyway. The image of Rose naked on the couch haunted me for the whole time I had to wait for the train.

"Mark, where the fuck have you been, you little fucking shit?" It was Harry.

"I have my own ticket to Boston and I'm not going with you, asshole!" I screamed back. "You can fuck anyone you want, but you'll never fuck me again."

Harry grabbed my arm, twisted it hard, and pulled me to my feet. The people in Grand Central looked on in horror. He forced me to walk up to the ticket counter with my arm twisted behind me and to cash in my ticket. Then he pushed me into the car and drove us to Boston.

I was addicted to the drama of it. Even with all the times Harry was unfaithful, I knew that he loved me more than anyone else. Fidelity wasn't a priority, it was only one of a dozen scenes in a play called Fucking Harry.

THERE WAS A GAY BAR in downtown Syracuse called Crotch Cave. It was just a dumpy little bar, but it was jumping and I was curious about the drag shows they had there on Sunday nights that attracted gays as well as straights. Back then seems as if all the gay people were either butch or fem. Harry and I had never thought of ourselves as a man and a woman. We were more like two brothers. I didn't know anyone else who was like us, and I was intrigued by these drag queens. I couldn't understand why anyone who was attracted to guys would want to have sex with someone who looked like a woman.

I ventured in with a girlfriend, Laura, to watch the drag show. Laura and I struck up a conversation with a group of guys we met there. Bill was a long-haired hippie whom I eventually slept with and Russian Cathy ended up marrying. Billy's cousin Peter was a drag queen and in hairdressing school. Peter's friend Danny Hart, also a queen, was seventeen, had just gotten his hairdressing license and was working at a salon in one of the toniest apartment buildings in Syracuse. After hearing all about Peter from Danny, I tried to convince Sylvia to get her hair done there.

"Mom, I met some guys who told me about a new hair salon, in the Regency Towers. Some women from temple go there, like Mrs. Kahn. You should go and get Danny to do your hair. I want you look to look chic like all those other women at temple." On the day of her appointment, we drove downtown. The salon was small with only about five stations. The fake French Provincial décor was plush, stuffy, and overdone. Danny greeted us at the door. He was short and skinny with blonde hair, and if you looked, you could see his plucked eyebrows from dressing in drag on the weekends. Sylvia didn't seem to notice and took to Danny almost immediately. Danny knew how to make Sylvia feel good. She loved going to him and he loved her.

I liked Danny, but I didn't think that he liked me. He seemed to think I was a tourist, saying, "You don't know what growing up poor is like. You're used to getting whatever you want. You think coming to gay bars and watching the drag shows is cool. Let me tell you, we know what we're destined for—a long miserable existence. That's all anyone who is gay can expect."

I was interested in Danny's lifestyle and that of the other drag queens, but I knew I was gay in a different way.

Sylvia came across an article in *The New York Times* about a trendy new salon in New York City. She said, "Mark, look at this. There's a place in the East Village on St. Mark's Place called Central Park Mall. It says here they specialize in cutting long hair. Your father would be so happy to see you with any kind of a haircut. It costs ten dollars."

Abe yelled, "Ten dollars! Are you crazy? I pay a dollar, seventy-five." Then in a softer voice, he said, "Well, anything is better than what he has."

I knew I wanted my hair cut like Mick Jagger or Jim Morrison. I had seen unisex shags on some Syracuse University kids and on Jane Fonda, but I didn't know how it was done. None of the shops in Syracuse were cutting hair in shags yet. At the time, St. Mark's Place had about five hair salons with hippie clientele. The first and most famous of these new unisex salons was Paul McGregor's, where Jane Fonda got her shag cut for the movie, *Klute*.

My parents sent me to New York. I walked into Central Park Mall. Ginny had recommended someone who worked there so I asked for him. "Is Jim working here today?"

The receptionist looked me up and down. I couldn't tell if she was bored, or just high. "Hold on and I'll see if he's around."

Someone who I guess was Jim came out. He had cool long reddish brown shaggy hair and he had the same half bored or half high look on his face that the receptionist did.

I looked around to see if I could get an idea of how I wanted my hair cut. When I asked Jim if he knew Ginny, he thought he remembered her. I liked the salon. It was different than the Regency Tower salon. It had exposed brick walls, antique barber chairs and gold leaf mirrors. You could smell the burning incense in the air. I sat down in the chair. My hair was a little past my shoulders at the time. It would've been longer, but I kept having to get it cut every time I was arrested. Jim asked me if I wanted my hair layered. I didn't know what that meant. So I said, "Just a little."

Jim started by layering it on the bottom. It didn't look much different, just flipped on the bottom, so I told him to cut bangs. Now, I looked like Marlo Thomas, "That Girl." I was afraid to let him cut anymore, so I told him that it was great just the way it was. I couldn't believe I had to go back home looking like that. Before I left I took a good look around. There were all these guys with long hair hanging around, drinking wine and smoking grass. Great music was playing and everybody looked really cool. I thought to myself, "I could do this!"

I returned to Syracuse with a new idea. I'd learn how to cut hair in this new, layered style, move to New York and work in one of those hip salons. I'd be on my own and I wouldn't have to answer to anyone. As soon as I returned, I called the Regency Tower and made an appointment with Danny.

"What the hell did you do to yourself, jerk? You look like That Girl."

"Thanks, Danny. I want you to cut the top short like the rockers."

Well, he cut it short all over, except the sides and back. Now I looked like Mia Farrow with fringe. As it grew out, I kept cutting the bottom and the top. Nobody but hairdressers at that time had blow dryers, so I used the vacuum cleaner hose to get the top to stand up. After a few months it started looking really great.

Everyone wanted his or her hair cut like mine, so I started cutting other people's hair. Kids came to my house after school and even their moms wanted me to cut their hair like mine. I charged three dollars a head for my vacuum cleaner cuts and for the first time in my life, I was making money doing something I loved. Sylvia was upset about all the hair on the bathroom floor, but she didn't want to discourage me.

I talked my parents into letting me go to beauty school at night. The school required the students to be sixteen-and-a-half years old, so that you wouldn't quit school. It didn't stop me from wanting to drop out, though. I was sixteen and a half and I knew you only needed to be sixteen to drop out without your parent's permission.

I'd had enough. I was already in beauty school at night. If I quit, I could go full time and move to New York City sooner. I couldn't picture myself in a conventional job, and I didn't need a high school diploma to be a hairdresser on St. Mark's Place. As I strode purposefully down the corridors of Nottingham High, some of my friends began to follow me down the hall. I stopped at my locker and removed all the books. I carried them in my arms and marched down the hall to the principal's office with my entourage trailing behind me. They all stopped at the door as I walked right past Mrs. Parker, the receptionist and straight into Mr. Braxton's office. I dumped my books onto his desk and announced, "I quit."

"What do you mean, 'you quit?' How about if we talk to your parents?"

"I know my rights. I can quit school when I'm sixteen and I don't need their permission."

Mr. Braxton looked like Sergeant Friday from "Dragnet." He called Mrs. Tremont, my art teacher into his office. I was considered the best art student in the school. Mrs. Tremont said, "Mark, what are we going to do with the ten foot high papier-mâché mermaid you made? It won't fit through the door."

Mrs. Tremont called me a "modern tragedy." When I got home, Mr. Braxton beat me to my house and was sitting at the kitchen table with my father. My father's eyes were watery and bloodshot.

"Mark, this is breaking my heart. My father died when I was seven years old, and left my mother with ten children. We didn't have any money and everyone had to work very hard to make ends meet. I couldn't go to college. We had no money. I had to go to work. You, on the other hand, can go to just about any college you choose."

I felt really terrible for my Dad, but not terrible enough. My mind was made up. I wasn't going back to school. Then Sylvia came home. I heard her car pull in the driveway and the side door by the kitchen slammed as she walked in. She looked at everyone seated at the kitchen table, and I could tell by the look on her face that she wasn't happy.

"Do you think you're going to hang around the house all day long doing nothing, wasting your life? I won't have it! I am not going to watch you throw your whole future out the window. I'm disgusted with you!"

After about an hour of circular discussion at the kitchen table, my parents and Mr. Braxton gave up. Sylvia told me I had to go to beauty school full time, but that's what I wanted anyway. She stopped speaking to me for about two months—not a word. She'd drive me to beauty school downtown on her way to work and pick me up later. At home she didn't speak to me either.

I had some trouble fitting in at the Contemporary Beauty School. The other students thought I was a spoiled Jewish kid. Most of the students were on welfare and took out student loans that they would be saddled with repaying as soon as they graduated. They resented me because my parents paid my tuition in full. I concentrated on doing well in beauty school and my efforts were rewarded almost immediately. I won the first place trophy in the beauty school competition in my first two weeks of school because Danny had coached me. This didn't make me any more popular.

While I was still in beauty school, Danny moved to New York City and got a job at Hair Power, right across the street from Central Park Mall where I had gotten my hair cut. My mother thought it fine for me to visit Danny in New York because she loved him. I went to Hair Power where he worked. He was glad to see me and introduced me to Carlo, the owner.

"Mark, how are you? You look great. Tell me how are things back home and how are Abe and Sylvia? Listen, tonight is the second annual gay rights march to commemorate the Stonewall. You want to come?"

The Stonewall riots broke out on June 27th, 1969. The New York City police had been raiding gay bars for years. The police would storm into the bars, arrest the queens and gays and dikes for lewd behavior and impersonating women, and then release them. The bars all paid off the police. The cops saw the queens as easy targets. They never in a million years thought they'd fight back. But the night of Judy Garland's funeral at a gay bar called the Stonewall Inn in Greenwich Village, the cops carried out their most famous raid. This time, the queens decided they'd had enough. They fought back against the police, throwing beer bottles and punching and kicking cops. It ended up in a huge riot that went on for several nights. Now every year, there is a gay civil rights march in Greenwich Village (and other locations around the world) marking the day when the gays fought back — and won. That night I met Danny and his friends. As we were marching down Fifth Avenue with all the other gays, people gathered along the curb and cheered us on. There were reporters and photographers taking pictures. One drag queen who was carrying a sign that said "Drag Queens Unite," caught her high heel on a metal grate and broke the heel off. She handed me the sign while she fixed her shoe. I saw a flash.

The next day Danny and I were at a newsstand and I was on the front page of the *East Village Other,* I was wading in the middle of the sea of drag queens carrying a huge sign saying "Drag Queens Unite."

I told Danny, "What if my parents see this?"

"Your parents don't read the *East Village Other*, you dickhead."

My only friend at Contemporary Beauty School was a young black woman. Gloria was was always trying to get me to go to church with her.

I said, "I'll make you a deal, Gloria, you come to temple with me and I'll go to your church."

She answered, "I have to ask my minister."

When I came home and told Sylvia about the deal, she said, "Just go to her church." She didn't want people in our synagogue to think I had a black girlfriend who wasn't Jewish.

I went to church that Sunday with Gloria. I did not know how to drive so she picked me up. Standing at my front door, she looked beautiful and seemed much too cheerful for such an early hour. I was not a morning person. She was dressed very conservatively. My eyes were bloodshot and I looked like a bum. Gloria and I said goodbye to Sylvia and got in her car. I didn't really know that much about the Pentecostal religion. I figured I could just sit in the back and stand up and sit down when everyone else did. To get to the church, we drove through a bad neighborhood on the south side of town. I was glad I was with Gloria because I wouldn't have wanted to be there alone and white on a Sunday morning. You could still see people stumbling home from the night before. We parked the car and walked up the long steps to the church. It was an old church with amber colored, stained glass windows. Everyone was black. When I walked in, the Pastor, Reverend Jones (the father of Grace Jones) shook my hand and welcomed me. There was no way I was going to fade into the woodwork. We all sat down and Reverend Jones came out to speak. His deep urgent voice resonated throughout the building, and after every line, the congregation shouted "AMEN."

The music began. It was not like the music at my temple. This music was jumping. In no time, the people were clapping and singing and standing up in the aisles. I thought to myself, "Wow, this is great—this is groovier than being Jewish." I stood up and started to boogie with them. Gloria was singing and moving her arms. All of a sudden things began to change. Some of the people around me started shaking and acting really strange, including Gloria. Everyone was shouting, "Jesus, Jesus, Jesus" over and over. Some were rolling on the floor. I got really freaked. Looking around, I realized I was one of the only sober people in the church. I thought 'These people are on drugs'. I also realized I had no way home.

After a while, things seemed to calm down. Gloria seemed coherent enough that I thought she could drive. I just wanted to get out of there as fast as possible, but she insisted that I meet with the pastor before I left. Gloria grabbed my hand and brought me up to Reverend Jones on the podium. I'll never forget his voice, like "the Great Oz had spoken." "Welcome to our church, son. Are you ready to accept Jesus Christ as your savior and be baptized in the name of the Holy Ghost?" He started to steer me towards a small swimming pool behind the altar. I was willing to do all kinds of things in my life—drugs, sex, but my Jewish upbringing was very strong. My mother kept a Kosher home. I knew this was wrong. There was no way I was going to do this, but I didn't want to embarrass Gloria. I told the Reverend I was Jewish.

"Jesus was a Jew," he answered.

I turned and said, "Tell my mother that!" But I liked him. He had found his faith in a weak moment, not in a strong one. Later when I met his daughter Grace Jones and her brother Christian who also cut hair in the city, I realized what a textured man he must have been.

I graduated beauty school shortly after that. Gloria took up a collection and presented me with fifty dollars from the other students. I really liked her and she was my only beauty school friend. At home, I had an announcement to make. I said, "Mom. Dad, now that I'm 17 years old and have my New York temporary hairdresser's license, I want to move to the city and nothing you can say is going to change my mind."

My parents were too tired to fight anymore. Abe said, "Mark, you're much too young to be out on your own in the big city. If you leave home, I won't give you a dime!"

"I don't care. I don't need your money. I have fifty dollars."

UTOPIA

Abe drove me to the train station and gave me one hundred fifty dollars. He told me to call him when I got there, if I needed more money. I had friends in New York. I was living out of a suitcase and staying wherever someone I knew would let me sleep. I had a friend who lived in the East Village with his wife and baby. I stayed on the floor of the baby's room next to the crib. There were roaches everywhere. On weekends, I stayed with a friend in the Bronx whose mom went to the country. I had to find a place of my own and I needed a job.

I went to Hair Power and asked Carlo if he'd give me a job.

Carlo was there in the front and he remembered me. "You're Danny's friend, right?"

I nodded.

"And you cut hair, right?"

I nodded again.

"You want a job?"

I nodded yet again.

"Start tomorrow." Carlo was a skinny, short Italian from the South Bronx. He had seven brothers, all of whom were killed by the mob. Carlo was a coke freak and his personality reflected his addiction. His periodic paranoid fits of rage were legendary. When I began, he was looking for an entire new staff. This is because he had fired the entire old staff just days before, as he often did when he was crashing from coke. He was volatile, unpredictable and everyone just tried to stay out of his way. His best friend was Monty Rock III, the famous hairdresser / nightclub performer who was always on Johnny Carson.

I told Carlo I was nineteen and had one year of experience. He led me to the back of the salon to the last empty work station and gave me the first walk-in customer—a tall, red-haired guy with long stringy hair. I cut it in my self-taught vacuum cleaner cut. When Carlo saw it, his face turned beet red.

"What the hell kind of shit is this, Blondie? Where did you work, anyway, in a dog grooming shop? As soon as I find someone else, you're outa here."

I just kept coming back to work every day, though, dodging Carlo, and trying to keep a low profile. I was doing a lot of speed at the time, so I improved quicker than I otherwise would have. Most of my clients were long-haired, hippie types who were cutting their hair for the first time and were so glad to leave with their hair still long; they were usually happy.

Shortly after I was hired, Carlo hired a new receptionist. Blanche Sands was black and spoke with a clenched-teeth WASPY accent. She always wore a bandanna. She was pretty, but always appeared stressed-out and worried. She chain-smoked Parliaments from morning to night. Her best friend was Betty Davis, Miles Davis' ex-wife. Betty was about 5'5" with a huge Afro that added about a foot to her height. She had caramel-colored skin and wore tons of turquoise jewelry with her vivid dream coat colors. She was voted Best Dressed

Underground Woman of the Year by the *Village Voice*, and was a powerful, funky vocalist in her own right. They credit her with inventing fusion rock. Blanche and Betty were both heavily into the band Santana. Blanche dated one of the back-up guitar players and Betty dated Gregg Rolie who was a founding member of Santana. Another friend of theirs, a light-skinned black girl named Devon, was one of the late Jimi Hendrix's girlfriends. They all talked about Santana and Hendrix. Jimi Hendrix's song "Dolly Dagger" was written about Devon. I'd overheard Blanche talking about Devon on many occasions. Devon was a junkie and hustled. She wore fur coats and blouses that showed her breasts. The line from the song, "She drinks her blood from a jagged edge" was about her. She died of an overdose during the filming of a documentary by the Maysles brothers about her withdrawal from heroin.

People hung out at Hair Power for hours—smoking weed, drinking wine, doing speed, listening to music. And talking. No one can gossip like someone between shampoos. But I was also paying attention, and feeling a new vibe. The hippie movement was giving way to the glitter rock and disco scenes. High-heeled boots and Rod Stewart hair were replacing beards and sandals.

Studio apartments in the West Village in 1971 went for about one hundred fifty dollars a month. I found a five-room apartment on 2nd Avenue and 4th Street, in the East Village for one hundred fifty dollars. It was a fourth-floor walk-up in a rundown building. It had one room with a toilet, a bathtub in the kitchen, and four other small rooms, all in a row with no hallway. It was called a railroad flat since you had to go through each room to get to the next. Only one room had windows looking down on 2nd Avenue. The other windows looked at a brick wall. Though run down, the building had high ceilings and beautiful old wood moldings. My father sent me the money for the first and last month's rent and the broker's fee, altogether four hundred fifty dollars. I had no furniture, so the building superintendent offered me an old bedroom set that had been left behind by a deceased tenant. Beggars can't be choosers, so I took it, mattress and all. It turned out to be a beautiful old Art Deco bedroom set.

My parents drove down with my old dog, Champ. My father loved that dog. The only artwork in their house were pictures of afghans with their manes blowing in the wind.

Abe and Sylvia bring some of my things I had left at home. They pulled up and took a good look at the neighborhood and the building where I had chosen to live. It was run down and dirty. The hallway smelled like stale urine. Abe carried some boxes upstairs and then just sat on the third floor landing. Champ was too afraid to go any further. Abe put his head in his hands and started to laugh. I have a feeling that before they left, Abe paid off the Italian couple who owned the first floor candy store to keep an eye on me, especially since Abe knew I had a sweet tooth. The couple were always watching what I was doing and offering unsolicited advice about who I should or shouldn't be hanging around with. They actually should've been more aware of their own people, because I knew for a fact that their nephew, Gino, who worked there, was dealing drugs he got from a doctor. He'd sit in the back room with bags of all different kinds of pills, uppers and downers, counting them for customers. He gave me whatever I wanted because he had the hots for me.

I got acquainted with the neighbors pretty quickly. I met two topless dancers named Astar and Alice from California. They lived on the next block and I'd to see them around all the time. They would also frequent the candy store. The owners of the candy store openly disapproved of my association with the strippers. Astar was a tall, blonde California chick with long legs. She had a variety of elaborate hairpieces, so her look was always changing. Alice was a bleached blonde with small, perky boobs.

There was an old building across the street called the Molly Picon Theater. Years ago it was a Yiddish Theatre, but now it featured local bands and performance art. "Sylvester," who later became a disco star, played there for a couple of months with a drag biker revue called the "Coquettes." From San Francisco, they all had tattoos, stringy hair and beards, and wore tutus, evening gowns and motorcycle jackets. Astar and Alice were friends with them and brought them over to my apartment to party. The girls always had lots of cash and we all did a lot of speed. I snorted crystal meth and popped Dexedrine pills and we spent a lot of time smoking cigarettes and not eating very much.

With all that speed coursing through my veins, I couldn't sit still. I painted my apartment three times because I changed my mind about the color. After scraping at the side of the windows, I exposed some nice shutters and in the wall was a brick fireplace that had been covered over with plaster. I ripped seven layers of linoleum off the floor and painted the floor black. I learned that amphetamines and home improvement go together.

Another friend, David Johnson, used to come into Hair Power all the time. He was six-foot-tall, stick-thin, light-skinned, bi-racial Englishman with a foot high Afro. I loved the way he talked. It was very hip to be English at the time. He was a clothing designer for Jumpin' Jack Flash and Granny Takes a Trip, hip clothing boutiques with stores in both London and New York City. Later in life, he moved back to England and designed the stage outfits the band "Kiss" was famous for. He always had on these great rock and roll outfits and high silver platform heels. He wore the complete Yves St. Laurent rhinestone collection on the lapels of his vintage sport jackets.

David was into downs. He'd come to my apartment while I was up for hours painting, speeding my brains out. He had a hard time standing up straight in his high heels because of all the downs he was taking. Then he'd blame it on the high heels. "It's the shoes; it's the shoes," he'd repeat into the night. David would pass out in a room painted one color and wake in the same room painted in another color. I credit David Johnson for introducing me to my friend Phyllis at Max's Kansas City. She was a wild party girl who loved to go to the clubs every night. At the same time, she was sensitive and compassionate. She would become one of my best friends.

I had been in my apartment about three months when I discovered that it was infested with bed bugs—I thought they were just in that rhyme, "Sleep tight. Don't let the bed bugs bite." I didn't think they were really real. I couldn't stand to live there any longer. I told Blanche Sands, the receptionist at Hair Power, about my dilemma. She took pity on me and said if I paid her rent, I could stay in her apartment. Her roommate, Betty Davis, was in California most of the time and if she came back, I could stay up the street with her friend Kenny Goldstein.

Blanche and Betty lived in "Twin Peaks" — a registered historic landmark—on Bedford Street in the West Village, just off Christopher Street. It was built by the city in the 1920s as artist housing. Century and resembled a Swiss chalet. The inside of the apartment was all paneled in dark wood and everything was built in. It looked like the captain's cabin of a pirate ship. On weekends, tourists tried to look in the windows to catch a glimpse inside. We had to have black out curtains. The apartment we lived in was only one room. I slept on the big bed and Blanche slept on the carpeted floor, except for the weekends Betty came to New York. Then I'd go to Kenny's up the street. Kenny's downstairs neighbor was Peter Allen, Liza Minelli's ex-husband. Peter was attracted to me from the beginning. Peter's roommate, David Smith, was a bartender at "The Ninth Circle." It was originally a Village steakhouse, but after a change of owners became one of the most famous gay bars in the city. We all used to hang out there and sometimes I'd run a tab and then just slip the money under their door to David.

Peter wasn't yet famous for his singing and songwriting talent, and was known for being Liza Minelli's ex-husband. I dropped by one night to leave Peter's roommate some money when he asked me in. Peter asked me to sit while he and his friends were watching Liza win the Academy Award for Cabaret. Another time I met her at the Ninth Circle. She tipped her chair back so far that she almost fell over backwards and everyone nearby scrambled to catch her before she hit the floor. She was pretty smashed and couldn't seem to stop giggling. Peter also came to the eighteenth birthday party that Blanche threw for me. I knew he wanted to sleep with me, but he was just too old, thirty or something. Maybe if he looked like Hugh Jackman.

I continued to stay with Blanche and work at Hair Power, but felt like I really should have a place of my own. One day, as I was cutting a client's hair and pondering my uncertain future, I looked up and freaked.

"Mark, man, how are you? It's been a while dude, but I've been abroad. The band has been touring the UK, Germany and France. I don't know if you've been following my success. We've got two hits on the top forty. No matter where I've been or what I've done, I've never forgotten you. I called your parents. They told me you were working here. Maybe we could see each other."

I was so shaken. Just seeing Harry Myers again made me feel faint. I said nothing. I was afraid to open my mouth.

Blanche chimed in, "Mark's staying at my place. Come over any time."

Harry started coming around to see me at Blanche's. He was still as big, blonde and beautiful as I remembered, but there was always a dark side to Harry, and I remained skeptical. He asked me to get an apartment with him. I was afraid to move in with him, but I couldn't stay with Blanche forever. So, Harry, who had changed his name to Chris Robison, and I got a large two bedroom on Commerce Street with a garden. I was now eighteen. I knew, however, that he'd changed. More often than not, he was prone to extreme mood swings. Then he quit his band and joined John Lennon's backup group, Elephant's Memory. He'd stay out into the wee hours of the morning with no explanation, or not come home at all for days at a time. He accused me of sleeping with everyone from Long John Baldry to David Johanson of the New York Dolls. He'd rage on about me coming home late from work or going out with friends.

Living with Harry was draining the life out of me. Sometimes I'd wake up and look at him and think how handsome, smart and cool he was and how lucky I was, an eighteen-year-old nobody, to be hooked up with him. I'd go to work and all I could think of was Harry. But I was haunted by the unsavory and dangerous things he did. I became addicted to the drama of the relationship. When things were good, when he showed affection towards me, I'd be walking on air. I felt like Harry was part of my soul. And then he'd bring home some thirteen-year-old young boy, starry-eyed in love with him and act as if it were nothing.

Our fights were legendary among the neighbors. It was not unusual to hear screaming, shouting, things being thrown out in the courtyard in the early hours of the morning. If Harry brought someone else home, I'd flirt with him until the boy would want to get it on with me. Then Harry and I would fight and argue for hours. I threatened to leave countless times, but even when I left, it was only for a few days. When I was gone, I'd walk around in a fog feeling disconnected and empty. Without him, I was nothing. When I would finally come to my senses and decide to end the relationship, he'd reel me back in again. He'd take me out with him to the clubs or to his gigs and introduce me as his boyfriend.

Harry was snorting speedballs—a combination of heroin and speed. Even though I was doing a lot of speed myself, I was mostly popping pills. When he'd crash from the drugs, Harry would beat me. And he started bringing home groupies. They were mostly twelve and thirteen-year-old boys.

I tried to stay out and away from Harry as much as I could. He was getting stranger and scarier all the time. He made his own album, all about loving young boys called "Chris Robison and His Many-Hand Band." No one bought it. I started to realize that Harry was really a pedophile. I met him when I was fifteen and now I was getting too old for him.

I confided in Alice and Astar. They told me to start going out to clubs with them and maybe I'd meet someone else.

On one of our nights out, we met a stunning, tall, thin, dark-haired guy named Dwain Flynn. He was from L. A., and about my age, and was Cherokee and Irish. He had incredible chiseled features and long, shiny, black hair. The girls and guys in the clubs drooled over him. I remember standing on the street with him when a bus full of schoolgirls passed. They were screaming out the bus windows for him.

Dwain told me that he and his boyfriend had a very volatile relationship. His boyfriend had beaten him on more than one occasion, when in fits of drunken jealous rage he accused him of being unfaithful. I felt a connection to Dwain. I felt we were both involved in these tragically romantic violent relationships and that we truly understood one another. We had sex once or twice and then just became good friends.

THE EARLY 1970S CLUB SCENE in New York was wild—each venue more elaborate and over-the-top than the next. There was Max's Kansas City, a rock and roll club where Andy Warhol hung out. It was also a favorite haunt of rock stars like David Bowie, Alice Cooper, Iggy Pop, the Rolling Stones, the New York Dolls and everybody who was anyone in the art and rock scene. Tamberlane was an uptown disco that was almost like a theme park. It was designed to look like Sherwood Forest. As you entered, you had to walk on a drawbridge, over a moat. The walls were covered with faux stone and foliage and there were huge tree trunks in the middle of the dance floor. Straights and gays and trans all danced together in these clubs. Jackie O came in one night with bodyguards. I guess she was slumming.

The people I met at the clubs were fascinating, unforgettable. One of the most outrageous characters was a friend of David Johnson. Her name was Potassa De La Fayette. This, I was told, was Spanish for whore. When she walked into a club, everyone turned to stare. Potassa was about six feet tall and a striking Latin beauty. She was a drag queen, but looked like a very tall beautiful woman. She was one of the first people to have silicone breast implants. Special clamps were required while sleeping to keep them from falling. She also had implants in her calves and cheeks. When Potassa walked into a club, all you saw was her striking beauty. She was photographed for *Vogue* seven times before they found out she was a man. All the top designers, Halston, Calvin Klein, Steven Burroughs, etc., made clothes for her. David Johnson gave me a vest once belonged to her. There were studs in the armpits and an array of studs down the back that drew everyone's eye on the dance floor.

Today people are much hipper and she would look more like a drag queen, but in the early seventies, no one had seen fake breasts before and to everyone I know she looked like a woman. She had her own groupies. The mafia opened a club and named it *Potassa*.

Potassa danced with her hand upon her temples and a hop up and down. It was the first "voguing" that Madonna would later copy. Everyone in the clubs imitated her dance, calling it "The Potassa." She talked in a smoky voice like a Spanish Zsa Zsa Gabor. Potassa fucked both girls and boys and had a twelve-inch dick. One night at Tamberlane, I saw a man pay one hundred dollars just to see it.

Alice introduced me to Long John Baldry, a British bluesman. He fell in love with me and took me to all kinds of clubs and bought me expensive clothes. He had some Ozzie Clark shirts that shrank in some Dry Cleaners so he gave them to me. I wore them until they were shreds. I took advantage of his generosity, but I had no desire to sleep with him. He was too old. I would pretended to pass out on Quaaludes at the end of an evening together so I wouldn't have to have sex with him. Once, he took me to see a strange lady performer named Bette Midler. This was before she played the Baths. No one really knew who she was. She told all these tit jokes that went over my head but were hilarious.

The New York Dolls would sometimes come over and party at my apartment. The Dolls never became a commercial success; most record companies were afraid of signing the band because of their outrageous cross-dressing and naughty language, but they did have a huge and dedicated cult following in New York City.

As outrageous as the personalities were and as much fun as everyone seemed to be having, there was also a sense of danger that permeated the atmosphere. At that time, many of the clubs were owned by the mob and there was much infighting over the lucrative cash disco business. I'd hear stories about bodies being found in the Meat Locker. One night in "The Jungle," a place near the 59th Street Bridge, gunfire broke out and came through one of the windows of the club. Everyone hit the floor. There was also a suspicious fire at Tamberlane.

Quaaludes were the drug of the hour. All of a sudden everyone was doing them, and you would often see club kids passed out on the dance floor, Smokey Robinson, Isaac Hayes and the O'Jays crooning in the background. One night, a girl I knew passed out from too many Quaaludes. Another girl went up to her, took off her shoes and tried them on. When she saw that they fit, she stole them. "Smiling Face, Back Stabbers" by the O'Jays was playing on the club's sound system.

I dealt Quaaludes to supplement my income and support my blossoming habit. I shopped at The Late Show, Once Upon a Time and down the street Happily Ever After. Vintage clothing boutiques had the variety I needed. My hair had a blue streak on one side. My high-heeled, snakeskin boots were custom made in England. I had an antique ocelot coat and I wore Indian scarves. Sometimes I'd buy 1930s dresses, cut them in half and make the top part a shirt and the rest into scarves. Tight straight-legged jeans were in—bell-bottoms were out. Once, while I was in Limelight on 7th Avenue, a photographer from *L'Uomo* (Men's Italian Vogue) photographed me and other club kids in one of my over-the-top outfits. When the edition was published, someone translated the caption under my photograph—it read "The Decadence and Depravity that New Yorkers have gotten used to." My parents thought this was great, because they couldn't read Italian.

I continued to work at Hair Power, partying 'til dawn every night, but the conditions at my job were miserable. Carlo had fired five complete staffs of people since I started to work there. He never fired me, but that's only because everyone was even more fucked up than I was. I was turning nineteen and I was already burned out. I moved back to Syracuse for a few months to save some money. But I returned to New York City as soon as I was financially able. I felt like a freak again when I was back in Syracuse. I felt one hundred years older than any of my peers, and I felt I really didn't fit in anywhere. My parents took one look at my blue hair and clothes and went ballistic. At Thanksgiving dinner, Sylvia told me to put a rinse in my hair to cover up the blue. When I refused, she said, "Sit on the left. At least your uncle can't see the blue streak." I told her if they couldn't accept me as I was, I just wouldn't come home anymore.

"Drama Queen," replied Sylvia.

I returned to New York City. My good friend Phyllis and I moved into a small apartment on McDougal Street. I went back to working at Hair Power, but I really hated it. I started looking for other ways of making money, like hustling. I knew a guy from the clubs named Orlando. He was street-smart and slick. He looked like he was about fifteen and he had a big dick, ten inches. The older men loved his boyish looks and his big dick. I watched him make so much money and thought maybe I could do that—if only I could make myself detached enough so that I didn't have to think about what I was doing.

One of my stripper friends, blonde Kathy (not to be confused with Spanish Kathy), was applying for a job as a massage girl and asked me to accompany her. She was dressed for the part in a short skirt and tall, black, shiny, high-heeled boots. Her dyed, black hair was cut short and her tight shirt showed off her voluptuous figure.

We took a cab together to a place called Club Utopia. The sign read "Beautiful Male and Female Models Give Sensuous Nude Body Rubs." I recognized the manager Chris, from the clubs. He asked if I was interested in working for him. "Mark, how are you? Come in man; don't be shy. We make really good money here—one hundred dollars a day plus tips and you don't have to do anything you don't want to. I guarantee it. Come on, let me show you around," he said convincingly.

That was more than I made in a week at Hair Power, before tips. He showed me into a small room off to the side. The place was really dark, even though it was mid-afternoon. The floors and walls were painted black with black light designs, and the place smelled of smoke. The Rolling Stones "Satisfaction" played in the background. "Now, don't be shy with me, Mark, take off your clothes and let me look at you," he said.

I mechanically slipped out of my tight black jeans and shirt. I took everything off but my underwear.

He encouraged me further, "Well, come on man. Let's see the goods."

I took off my underwear and I stood there with my eyes averted under his stare. He told me I was hired. He herded me over into a sitting room with red velvet pillows and shag carpet. Kathy was smoking a cigarette and there were more boys and girls on the couch. Customers choosed whom they wanted: a girl, a guy or both. Some men wanted to watch the guys have sex with their wives. Some people brought uniforms for them to wear. There was a flat fee per person and a fifty-fifty split with the house and a tip. I lasted only a day. I took a Quaalude to relax me, and then I took another one. I woke up making out with another model / massage boy named Fran Z and was fired on the spot.

I didn't want to go back to Hair Power, so I tried to make a go of it on the street. I took a shower, popped a lude and took a train up to 53rd and 3rd. This was a famous hustling block. I had to do this stoned. I walked up to the corner. There were lots of other young guys and older men hanging around. Nobody talked. I just stood there hypnotized by the oncoming headlights. Someone pulled over and opened the passenger side door of a station wagon. I got in. He looked about fifty to fifty-five years old, balding and lived in Queens. A black poodle yapped away in the back seat. I couldn't believe I was actually doing this. We parked the car in front of an old bar on 56th Street. The annoying poodle stayed in the car while we went in. We both sat at the bar and drank beer as Donna Summer crooned in the background "Oooh, I feel love, I feel love, I feel love, I feel love, I feeeeeel love."

I did feel no love. After about four beers and some totally insipid conversation, we left and got back into his car. He asked me pee into a bottle that he had underneath the seat, shook my hand good-bye and gave me fifty dollars. I stuffed the fifty dollars into my pants pocket and walked home. The next time I picked up an ugly guy and went to a hill house in Brooklyn. All I could do was lay there and let him do me.

I tried my hand at 53rd Street one more time and picked up a real hunk, who I would've done for nothing. I really wasn't cut out for this. Abe and Sylvia would be so ashamed of me, and I was still hanging on to the illusion of finding my soul mate.

My hustling career was over.

I was back in my old bedroom again, in "Zero-Cuse" with Abe and Sylvia. I took a job at Hair Zoo—a hair salon on Marshall Street, on the small main commercial block in the heart of the university campus. The owner of Hair Zoo, Joe Burke, was tall and thin with dark hair and lots of hair on his chest and arms. He was straight and liked to hang out in the few disco clubs that Syracuse had.

I became something of a celebrity at the salon having left at such a young age to live in New York City. I liked my job and I met a lot of kids from the university who came up and hung out at Hair Zoo. I started drinking a lot because it was hard to get drugs in Syracuse and when you could get them, they weren't very good. Everyone there drank a lot.

My parents were very happy to have me home, at least Abe was. Sylvia had a tough time dealing with me. She thought I was too wild and she'd become accustomed to the peace and quiet while I was in New York. Now, people would call me at all hours and I know she felt my life was out of control. I knew my parents were trying to figure out if I was gay or straight—at least I thought that this is what they were always worrying about. I was always hanging around a lot of girls though, so they were able to continue rationalizing my behavior.

"Well, he always has a girlfriend," Abe would say and there was one girl, Nan, who I though I wanted to marry. She was model-thin, flat chested and pretty. It was easy to have sex with her because she had the body of a boy. She was a lot of fun, and my parents liked her, but she wasn't Jewish and they thought I was still much too wild to get married.

A few times Nan and I went to a local watering hole called the Orange. Sometimes we would meet up with a young student there named Stan. We would drink with him and then go back to his apartment for a nightcap. One night I pretended to pass out. Nan tried to wake me, but I made believe I was sleeping too soundly. Stan urged her to go home and let me sleep it off. When the door closed behind her, Stan and I went into his bedroom and fucked until dawn. Nan and I broke up. I did not want to keep ruining these girls' lives.

One weekend, my parents were at a party and I was home alone in the house. I was watching TV and drinking beers. I felt alienated from everyone and everything. In New York, I had freedom and glitz and parties and I was free to be myself, but I had no stability or boundaries. Here in Syracuse, I had the security of my family whom I loved and who I knew loved me, but my parents didn't truly know me. If I was going to stay here, I had to be able to be myself. That meant telling my parents I was gay. I know people who have never told their families and basically lived their lives as a lie.

I was lucky enough to have parents who were more open-minded than most.

That night, after one-and-a-half six packs of beer, I decided this was the time to tell them. I was nineteen years old. Abe and Sylvia came home in a good mood. I told Sylvia I had to tell her something. She looked very worried. She probably thought I was going to tell her I was in some kind of trouble.

"What is it, Mark? Have you been drinking?"

"Mom, I think you need to know something about me. I'm bisexual." I don't know why, but I just couldn't say 'gay'.

She just looked at me, confused. She said, "Is that all? I thought you were going to tell me something really horrible." She turned and walked away. She didn't' even tell my father, but I was sure she'd tell him later.

My father liked having me around and we had become close. He told me if I went back to New York, I wouldn't get a dime, but if I stayed in Syracuse, he'd help me. I started looking at Abe differently. Before it was always my mother I was close to, confided in. Abe was always very distant, but now they seemed to have switched roles.

I found an apartment in a new high-rise building in downtown Syracuse. It felt a little more like living in New York and I didn't have to fight with my parents. Every week I turned over my paycheck to my father. He paid all my bills for me and made up for any deficits. He wanted to know where every penny I made was spent. Every Wednesday we picked up my Aunt Belle and went grocery shopping and then to dinner. Abe bought my weekly groceries and I think this set-up really made Abe feel in control of me.

My mom, whose health was always poor, was diagnosed with breast cancer. She had to have one breast removed and a series of radiation treatments. Abe was so worried and concerned about her. He told her that he loved her so much that he still wanted to continue to sleep with her, but Sylvia couldn't handle the feeling of embarrassment at the mutilation her body had suffered. She began sleeping in the spare room. After seeing the way my father loved my mother I remember thinking that no one will ever love me like my parents loved each other. I felt that, being gay, I was somehow not entitled to that kind of love.

Tom worked at Syracuse University as a food service manager in the Haven Hall Dormitory. He was tall with dark, curly hair and was of Scottish descent. He looked somewhat like a young Sean Connery. He slept with me at my apartment almost every night for a year, but we didn't live together. He had his own place where he kept all his belongings. As in every relationship I'd had up to this point, I became bored with the sex.

One night Tom came over after hitting his usual nightspots. I was sitting on the bed crying inconsolably. My cousin Scotty who was going to University of Miami had killed himself. He had overdosed on Quaaludes. In his suicide note, he wrote that he thought he'd been rejected from getting into medical school. Scotty's death shocked me, and my family was devastated. I felt sick with guilt and sorrow. I was so much wilder than he was—it should have been me. At Cazenovia Lake we loved acting outrageously to baby sitters my Uncle hired. We blew up the motor in my boat, anything to discourage them from taking the job so we could be left alone. We were the same age and both of us adored our grandmother Fanny. Although he was blood and I was adopted she favored me. He tried to take her to lunch one day. "I'll only go if Markie goes," she told him.

"You wouldn't go if it were just me?" Scotty said.

"One grandson is going to be a lawyer. You are going to be a doctor. When I'm dead I won't need a lawyer or a doctor. A hairdresser, I could use."

Shortly after Scotty's death, tragedy struck my family again. My Grandmother Fanny, my savior and guardian angel, died. The services were held at Birnbaum's Funeral Home—the place where every Jew in Syracuse is buried. The funeral took place on a cold day in October. I went with Abe and Sylvia and we saw all kinds of strangers there. Many of the people were Jewish war veterans holding little Israeli flags. There were about two hundred people there. The Jewish community really loved Fanny. She had devoted her life to serving and bringing Jews together, especially the older immigrants coming from Eastern Europe. She was President of Hadassah, Jewish War Veterans Women's League, and she started the Syracuse chapter of Meals on Wheels and worked at the Red Cross. I thought I'd be sadder at Fanny's death, but I wasn't. Despite the pain of losing Scotty and Fanny, life went on.

My relationship with Tom was beginning to get boring. I thought if I expanded my sexual horizons, it would add some spice to our love life. I started reading Penthouse Forum about these straight couples that were into swinging. I suggested to Tom that we try it. He was quite receptive to the idea, which, of course, made me rethink my suggestion. I felt that I was better looking than Tom, but he was much more masculine and outgoing. We planned a trip to Provincetown. I wanted to go somewhere where no one would know me and if the experience turned out to be a fiasco, I'd never have to see them again. We went to a bar called the Moors where the music blared and strobe lights rotated hypnotically. Within a few minutes of sitting down at the bar, Tom had engaged a dark-haired guy sitting next to him in a conversation. He began to rub this man's shoulders and neck, and the guy was quite obviously enjoying it. I felt jealousy rising up in my blood. I was afraid of losing Tom.

"Tom, I want to go home."

"Okun, relax, we only just got here. Hang out a little."

The dark haired guy asked Tom if we came here together.

I said, "Yes, we're together, and we were just leaving." I grabbed Tom's coat and his arm and pulled him toward the door. He shot me a look of disgust, pulled the jacket from my hands.

"You know, Okun, you don't know what the fuck you want. First, you suggest we come here for some fun and then you're pissed off and making a scene. Give me a break, man, and figure out what the fuck you want."

The ride home was icily quiet. At home, I told him I didn't want an open relationship; I just wanted him. We broke up a couple of weeks later. The next Wednesday I was out for my usual grocery shopping and dinner with my parents and aunt. Tom and I were still talking back and forth, and I thought there might be hope of getting back together. I got up from the table, went to the pay phone, and called him. We got in a huge fight. When I returned to the table, I felt like I was going to cry. I grabbed my father's keys off the table so I could run to the car and cry without anyone seeing me.

"What's wrong with him?" Abe yelled.

"He had a fight with his friend," replied Sylvia.

"So what!" Abe yelled.

This is when my mother told my father I was gay, my aunt later told me. I had always assumed Sylvia told Abe this when I first admitted it to her. He never said a word to me about this conversation. The only way I knew it took place is because my aunt told me about it. After that, Abe seemed more loving towards me than ever. Right around this time he retired and he used to stop in to see me at Hair Zoo. In fact he came around constantly and I was embarrassed to have my little father always hanging around in front of my clients.

I was too old to have my dad run my financial life. I was making more money now, so I opened my own checking account. Abe had trouble letting go. I'd see his car drive by every night around 10:00 pm to see if my lights were on.

On a Thursday afternoon in October, Abe and Sylvia had just come home from shopping. Abe went upstairs to his dressing room to change. They were supposed to go out to dinner that night with Uncle Carl (the neighborhood bookie) and his wife, Aunt Mindy. When Abe didn't come downstairs for over an hour, Sylvia got worried. She found him collapsed on the dressing room floor. She called an ambulance, and he was rushed to Upstate Medical Center. Uncle Carl called me at Hair Zoo. He said, "Mark, you must come right away. Your dad suffered a massive cerebral hemorrhage. We're at the hospital."

I met Sylvia in the ER. The doctor explained to us, "Your husband is brain dead. Although he may stay alive on life support, he will just be a vegetable." My mother made the difficult decision to take him off life support. First Scotty, then Fanny and now Abe. Sylvia was devastated. She sobbed uncontrollably and refused to leave his bedside. Ten days later Abe was declared dead. He never cashed his first Social Security check.

I went to Birnbaum's to pick out the casket. My mother couldn't function. I thought of the rare coins I had stolen to go to California. I saved for years to replace them. I held the coins tightly in my hand as I went up to say goodbye to my father, and placed the coins in the casket.

The rabbi told us we didn't have to sit Shiva for seven days because we sat at his bedside for ten days and mourned then.

I drank my way through all this grief. I blamed my escalating drinking problem on all the loss I was experiencing. The truth is, I was worried about becoming an alcoholic. I read in a gay magazine about Gay AA and wondered if that could help me.

New Year's Eve was only a week away. Tom asked me to go with him to a party. I had hoped this meant he still loved me and wanted to get back together.

"Why didn't you call me when my father died? I was so alone. I could have used someone to talk to."

"I don't know. I just felt strange calling."

I wasn't really accepting that. On New Year's Eve, we left together for the party. Tom looked very handsome, like a waiter, dressed in black pants and a white shirt. He gave me an expensive antique black onyx Art Deco desk set as a Christmas gift. I was encouraged by the gift. At the party, Tom started flirting with Trent, who was from Syracuse, but had moved to L.A. and was visiting his parents for the holidays. Without saying a word to me, Tom and Trent left. I was devastated. I finally realized that Tom really didn't love me. I felt so betrayed. Betrayal is the most painful feeling of all. That is why they say that divorce is worse than death.

I was so angry with Tom I stayed up all night drinking. Later at a bar, I picked up a young hot, blonde guy named Chris. Around 6:00 a.m., I drove to Tom's apartment complex with Chris in the car. I pounded on Tom's door. When he appeared in his bathrobe he was rubbing sleep from his eyes. Something in me just snapped and I hauled off and punched him in the nose and smashed the Art Deco desk set he had given me on the floor. I stomped outside to find Tom's Volkswagen Beetle in the parking lot. It was snowing heavily. I reached in and opened both side doors of the VW bug and got into my car and crashed into his opened doors using my car as a battering ram to bend his doors backward. Chris stood by in horror. The next day, Tom had to drive all the way to the body shop with both doors wide open.

I was so embarrassed by what I had done. Chris must have told everyone I was a lunatic. I didn't go to work all week. When I finally got the nerve to leave my house, I drove all the way to Utica to go out on Saturday night where no one would know me.

I confided in my mother.

"No one man or woman is worth it, dear," she said.

A psychologist lived in my building. I asked him to refer me to someone I could talk to. He referred me to Dr. Binder, a psychiatric social worker who specialized in counseling gay patients. After only a few sessions with Dr. Binder, we came to the conclusion that Syracuse was just too small for me. He didn't know if I was an alcoholic or not, but he said help was always there if I needed it.

I was never truly happy in Syracuse. I had only stayed to please my father and now he was gone. My mother realized this and told me to move back to New York. She said, "If you stay, it will be for me. I'd rather have a wonderful long distant relationship with you than have you resent me if you stay."

NIGHTS AT THE SAINT, SUMMERS ON FIRE ISLAND

Many of the friends I had made during my last stay in the city didn't want to bother with me since I'd gone back home. They thought I wasn't cool or tough enough to stick it out without running home to my parents. Only Dwain and Phyllis welcomed me back. I was starting to realize who my real friends were. Dwain had gone off to Paris and become a successful model. He recorded a dance single that was a hit with the Paris teenyboppers. He also slept with David Bowie. His striking good looks opened a lot of doors for him and now he was being *kept* by an older, very wealthy lawyer for a major American oil company. He took me to La Mouche and Les Jardins and would sometimes stuff a one hundred dollar bill in my pocket for drinking money. Everyone wanted to be near Dwain. It seemed like they couldn't wait to spend their money on him and I gladly tagged along. Dwain loved me and I was glad that such a glamorous person wanted me to be his friend.

While in Syracuse, I had become friendly with Mark M., Phil and Milton. These three queens formed their own posse—I called them My Evil Stepsisters. We often went clubbing together even though the gay bar scene in Syracuse was small, incestuous, catty and everyone was always gossiping about each other.

Mark M., despite his nice build and good looks, was terribly insecure. When we went to the bars, he wouldn't talk to anyone. He was too busy sizing everyone up and judging whether they were good enough for him or he was good enough for them. The end result was that he usually ended up alone. Milton was from the Onadaga Reservation. His parents were very wealthy. They owned a gas station and a western wear store. Because first nation members didn't collect sales tax, everyone bought their gas and cigarettes there and his family became millionaires. Phil was always overweight and was the nicest of the three.

I had mixed feelings about the three of them moving to New York. It would be sort of reassuring to have them around, but at the same time, it felt like they were bringing all of the neurotic, small town shit with them.

I rented an apartment on St. Mark's Place in a clean and well-kept building but on a slightly seedy block. It had a brick wall in the living room and a working fireplace. I found a job at a neighborhood salon on 36th and 3rd with the name Great Heads. They got phone calls all the time asking if we gave "great head."

I thought if I could just make enough money to pay my rent, go out dancing and have sex with someone hot once in a while, my life would be satisfying. I didn't believe I had enough talent to make the big money, and because I thought I was just average, not strikingly gorgeous like Dwain. I knew love was something I dared not hope for.

One Saturday night, I was out barhopping by myself. I had quit drinking after I bashed in Tom's car doors. I was walking from one boring bar to the next when a young girl came barreling through the door of a warehouse building I was passing on West Street near 12th Street and nearly knocked me over. She wore sweatpants, sneakers and a headband like a tennis player.

She wiped her forehead, which was glistening with sweat, and was breathing heavily. She said, "Wasn't that the best music you've ever heard in your life?"

"I don't know what you're talking about, what music?" I answered, confused.

"Weren't you in there dancing?"

"No, where?"

She ran her fingers through her short, tousled hair and said, "Come on, just pretend you're with me and I'll get you in. The bouncer will think you've been in there already."

I walked in the door and was stopped dead in my tracks by the sight of about three hundred gorgeous men and not more than ten women gyrating to blasting, mind-blowing, great music. The guys all had their shirts off and were covered with glistening sweat. There seemed to be a sheet of steam flowing down from the ceiling. Later I found out that this phenomenon was due to a bizarre convection pattern created by the large amount of heat and humidity pouring off the dancers. I couldn't believe it. I had never been in a club like this before. Most of the places I frequented were either large, glamorous discos with a small sprinkling of gays or bisexual men or small gay bars.

The place was very sparsely decorated and unlike most clubs, they served no alcohol; there was only a juice bar. It was almost like a gymnasium with platforms all around the side and a big dance floor. The awesome lighting arrays played on the painted walls making the room seem like it was pulsing with the speedy bass beat of the disco mixes.

Some twelve mirrored balls, in clusters on the ceiling, created complex, mind-bending patterns throughout the room. The DJ was spinning and remixing on the turntables and the sound system was like nothing I had ever heard before. Disco had been taken to a new level. It was an athletic sport.

My head started bopping and my body started shaking. I didn't care that I was alone. I jumped up on a platform and started shimmying up and down, like it was my own personal stage. Other people barely noticed me. I knew most were on drugs, but I didn't care. Some were snorting amyl nitrate, or poppers. Without drugs or booze, I was having the time of my life. It was a religious experience not unlike the spirit-filled Pentecostals. I danced until dawn and when I finally went outside, the light seemed surreal. I didn't know what happened to me. The name of the club was 12 West.

In the mid-70s, there seemed to be a mass migration of thousands of young, hot, gay men to Greenwich Village. I had never been in a place where gay men were in the majority. The exclusively gay disco scene was exploding and the competition was cutthroat. Everyone wanted to go to the hottest club.

In order to generate interest and make a name, clubs would limit their membership and make it very difficult to get in. True to human nature, everyone wanted what he couldn't get. Flamingo was a very exclusive and in-demand dance club. It was like 12 West, but you had to be a member to get in and memberships were nearly impossible to get. Someone had to die before a new membership would open up.

Mark M., Phil, Milton and I traveled in the same circles, but my evil stepsisters were always able to get in places I couldn't. They'd always leave me in the dust as they ran off to the ball. They got the older guys they dated to take them to Flamingo and they would never ask me.

In some ways, young gay men are like high school girls trying to belong to the "in" crowd. I believe this is because they never experienced appropriate socialization in their teens. When you are a gay boy in school, pretending that you like girls, you aren't really having the feelings that come with it. So, when you're older and realize it's men you're attracted to, you have those emotions for the first time. The gay scene was and is very status conscious. In the clubs, the hottest, richest, most gorgeous men were at the top of the food chain in gay society and everyone wanted to be there. Just like straight society, I guess.

I heard a rumor about the renovation of the old Fillmore East Theater on 2nd Avenue and 6th Street. I used to go there with Harry in my hippie days. Bruce Mailman was going to pour six million dollars into it, rename it "The Saint," and turn it into the biggest and hottest gay disco in the world. I went to see it and it looked incredible. I joined immediately. At this point, it was relatively easy to obtain a membership, since it wasn't due to open for six months. I got a cool plastic membership card with a picture of rays of light on it and a floor plan of the building. You were supposed to study the floor plan, I guessed, so that if you got too stoned, you wouldn't get lost.

I showed the card to my friends. Mark M. said to me, "No one's going to go to this new club, Mark. Flamingo is a New York institution, and there isn't room for two big clubs in the city."

On September 20, 1980, I went to opening night by myself (Mark and Milton went to Flamingo). The Saint was incredible. As I walked in the front door, there were industrial size coatrooms on either side. Most men, after they checked their coats, were in tight, short-sleeved, t-shirts or were bare-chested. Once inside, I walked down a long ramp. The walls were all charcoal gray and there was a huge banquet and bar in front, with two metal staircases on either side. The banquet table had fresh fruit and the bar served only juices and Rolling Rock ponies.

The second floor had a huge, 4,800 square foot dance floor and a legendary, 76-foot high dome that could be either transparent or opaque. A giant lighting tower with nearly 1,500 fixtures rose up from the center of the dance floor. Topping the lighting tower was a planetarium that projected images of the starry, night sky or sunrise on the huge dome over the dance floor. There was a massive sound system that employed nearly five hundred speakers.

During live performances, panels of the dome opened and performers like Viola Wills or Tina Turner materialized out of thin air. It was like nothing I'd seen before or since. The record companies knew that if a song was a hit in gay clubs, it would surely be a hit in straight clubs. Gay men have been the purveyors of good taste since the beginning of time.

The third floor balcony, carpeted in gray, wall-to-wall banquettes was where you went to have sex. Towards the middle of the evening, to change the mood and effect, they opened a hidden door at the top of the dome and a gigantic mirrored ball would drop down with lights bouncing off in all directions, adding to the surreal symphony.

I looked across the dance floor at all the gorgeous men dancing, thousands of them, each more beautiful than the next. My parents never told me about this—I thought it was the eighth wonder of the world. This must be why God put me on this planet.

The Saint became my life. When I got home after opening night, Mark and Milton dropped by my apartment. Mark told me that Flamingo was dead. The Saint had completely wiped it off the map. Shortly after that, both 12 West and Flamingo closed and Mark begged me to take him to The Saint with my membership card. Now I had it over Mark and Milton. Phil had married a Puerto Rican guy and had moved to the Bronx. Having found love, he had it over all of us.

I was still afraid to drink but after hours clubs at the time were juice bars. Drugs, however, were always readily available. I started taking diet pills to keep awake all night so I could dance until dawn like everyone else. So, I needed Quaaludes to bring me down after a long night of speeding and MDA.

I met Ron, whom I knew to be a drug dealer. Ron didn't trust anyone else and would only sell the drugs to me, so I took orders. Mark, Milton and the people from my salon would place their orders with me once a week. I would call Ron and arrange to come by his apartment. I'd have a laundry list of everyone's pharmaceutical requests and I'd leave with a paper bag full of drugs.

I worked all week, went to the gym, pumped iron, saved all my money, and stayed sober all week long. But on Saturday evening all bets were off. I often went on weekend binges that would keep me up for two days at a time. It's a good thing The Saint was only open on Saturday and Sunday. I needed Monday and Tuesday to recover.

On a typical Saturday evening, I would leave work with my week's pay and my bag of drugs. I went home, took a hit of speed so I wouldn't be hungry and my stomach would be nice and flat. I'd clean and rearrange my house like a maniac and set out fresh flowers, in case I got lucky and brought someone home. Around 1:00 a.m., I'd snort some MDA. I'm not sure exactly what MDA had in it, but it was a mild hallucinogenic—like mescaline mixed with amphetamines. The powdered form of Ecstasy made you feel very sensual, and if you snorted a small quantity a little at a time, you could control the intensity of the high throughout the night. I went to The Saint around 2:00 am and snorted some more. I wore my best, faded jeans and took off my tight t-shirt once I started dancing. My friends and I danced and tripped on the MDA all night long. Around 6:00 am the music slowed down. This down tempo, morning music was called "sleaze." It was my signal to pop a Quaalude to bring me down and make me horny. Many times I got lucky and brought home a hunk.

One memorable guy who I met at The Saint was George Magill. I was dancing when I caught his eye across the room. He was 6'4" and looked like Lyle Waggoner from "The Carol Burnett Show." He made his way across the dance floor towards me. He reached over to me, picked me up in the air and swung me around, and then kissed me on my mouth. I wasn't at all used to this, since I was tall too. We dirty danced all night and then went home to his place.

George was an actor. He was on a popular TV commercial where he played Superman. He was clever and charming, although quite full of himself. Sex with George was good, not because he was good at it, but because he was so good to look at. He was older than I was and more mature. He seemed to like me and we started dating. Gay men almost always sleep together first, and if the sex is good, they start dating. It's not a good system, but that's the way it is.

I couldn't wait to bring him around and show him off to my evil stepsisters, Mark, Phil and Milton. Flamingo was having a big closing party to mark its last night of being open to the public. George said he wanted to go and told me I could bring a few friends over to his chic apartment in Gramercy Park for drinks and we could all go together. I asked the Evil Stepsisters. I couldn't wait to see the looks on their faces when they saw George. When we got to George's apartment, the boys got very quiet. They were all jealous. We sat around and had a few drinks. Eventually, we all went out to Flamingo together. It was a dead zone, but I was glad I finally got to see it before it closed. We didn't stay long; then we all headed uptown to The Saint.

I also went to mixed discos like Studio 54. I was able to get in because I knew Steve Rubell from the gym. I had to wait at the corner of 8th Avenue until Steve came out and saw me standing alone, away from the crowd; otherwise, he wouldn't notice me among the sea of faces waiting to get in. Steve would come down and motion to the doorman to let me in, and the crowd would part, like the sea for Moses.

I had heard all about summers on Fire Island—how the partying went on for days—but I had yet to experience the hedonism. In June, 1978, Mark M., Phil and Milton needed another person to help pay for the place they wanted to rent, so they asked me. They went Friday taking the Fire Islanders' Bus, a bawdy shuttle service that stopped at several Manhattan corners and ended at the ferry dock. It was the only ground transportation which had flight attendants. I couldn't go with them because I had to work on Saturday, so I said I'd meet them there Saturday night.

Milton said, "Okay, we rented a room in Cherry Grove. You'll have to catch the Islander's Bus from the city to the Ferry in Sayville, Long Island. Then, you'll catch the boat to

Cherry Grove and we'll be there to meet you when you get off. Remember to take the right ferry. It has to say Cherry Grove."

Right before I left, Mark M. called me at work and told me they had found a better room in Fire Island Pines. Now I was to get on the boat to The Pines, not Cherry Grove.

The Fire Islanders' bus catered to the weekend partiers and served drinks en route. I sat down next to a nice old man and we struck up a conversation. He told me about all the great places on Fire Island and that he had been going there for years. He told me that the origin of Fire Island's name is uncertain to this day. Some think it was due to an old-time mapmaker's transcription error that misread "Five Islands," the number of small islands then at the mouth of the western inlet to Fire Island. Others believe that pirates once roamed the Island's shores. They would build fires on the beach at night in hopes of luring ships aground on the shoals to plunder them.

My seat companion asked me if I wanted a drink. I figured one beer couldn't hurt me. It was a pretty long ride and I was kind of nervous about not knowing where I was going or what to expect when I got there. I had two more beers, and then right before we got to the ferry, I popped a Quaalude.

In my relaxed state, I couldn't remember whether to take The Pines or the Cherry Grove boat. I picked the Grove. The ferry ride across the bay was beautiful. The sun was just setting over the water. I sat on the top deck and watched all the people. The smell of gasoline on water made me think of my childhood summers in Cazenovia. When we arrived at Cherry Grove, the other passengers scurried off to their destinations. I looked around for Mark and Phil. Finding a pay phone, I searched my pockets for change and picked up the receiver. Realizing I had no idea who to call or where Mark had rented the room, I slammed down the phone. I must have looked upset because a well tanned man in shorts and sandals said "Is something wrong? Do you need help or something?"

"I was supposed to meet some friends, and I think I got on the wrong boat. Now I'm not sure where to go or how to get there," I said.

"They're probably in The Pines," he said, adjusting his glasses and giving me a once over.

"How do I get there?"

"There aren't any cars on the island. The streets are wooden walks. You have to walk through the woods or take a water taxi."

"How long does it take to walk from here to The Pines?"

"About fifteen minutes. It's not far, but when you start walking from one town to the other, the boardwalk ends at the woods. It gets confusing and it's easy to end up on the wrong path. Do you want me to walk you, so you don't get lost?"

"Okay."

We started walking down the wooded walks with beachy names. Many people breezed by, dragging their grocery-filled red wagons, or jogged past in shorts and sandals. My legs were like rubber from the combination of alcohol and Quaaludes. As we walked inland, away from the shore, the wooded area on either side of the path became very dense. I could hear voices coming from the woods. I looked more closely and realized that the woods were pulsating with hot man-on-man sex—in every corner, next to every bush, in couples and groups, men of all sizes and shapes were fucking and sucking. I couldn't see any faces because of the darkness. I could just make out the outlines of peoples' bodies. I wondered why anyone would want to have sex with someone if they couldn't even see their face or body. These people could be having sex with someone ugly and not even know it! I was both repulsed and turned on at the same time. My parents would certainly not approve of this place.

After a few minutes of walking, my trusty guide started groping me. I was afraid he would leave me stranded, so I tried to placate him until I found my friends. "Listen, man, maybe we'll get it on later, but I really need to find my friends first."

"That's cool. We're not far—just keep walking down the path as it veers to the left."

As we walked onto the boardwalk and came out of the woods, I saw the lights just ahead. There was a beautiful harbor with yachts, restaurants and bars and small boutiques. The bizarre experience in the woods had sobered me up some and I realized I was hungry. We found an outdoor restaurant on the second floor of a disco overlooking the harbor. We sat down and ordered. As I looked over the balcony, I spotted Mark and Milton down by the water. I didn't want to lose them so I grabbed my bag and ran down the stairs, leaving my guide with the tab.

"Mark, Milton—wait!"

"Where were you, you stupid queen? We waited for over two hours."

"I guess I got on the wrong boat."

"You faggot. Well, what do you think, isn't this place fabulous?"

"Fabulous, girlfriend!"

"Come on, we'll show you where the room is and you can change and put your stuff away."

We changed and hung out for a while before going back to Cherry Grove to dance at the Ice Palace. In my haste to put my things together, all I had brought to wear was a pair of gauze pants that were too big and I didn't want to wear underwear because it showed through the pants. I had to put a safety pin in the waist of my pants to keep them up. We got to the Ice Palace around 1:00 am It was a huge, open-air dance bar at a hotel. The club opened out on to the pool outside. I recognized a lot of guys from The Saint, which was closed for the summer, dancing amongst a crowd of hip, straight people from Ocean Beach and Long Island. We all danced to the blaring beat of the music. At one point in the evening, my pants fell to the ground while I was dancing. In a typical New York way, no one seemed to notice except the guy I was dancing with.

"What do you do for an encore?" he said.

We heard a large commotion. Everyone began to move towards the large outside bar which overlooked a swimming pool. From the boardwalk in the direction of the beach a gorgeous, Spanish woman in a white Halston dress rode up to the wide entrance door of the Ice Palace on a beautiful gray horse. Everyone stared transfixed. I strained my tired eyes. As she came into focus it was Potassa! She gracefully dismounted from her white mare with two handsome guys helping her down and she began lip-syncing a well-known sleaze song: "Take off your make-up and let your hair down."

The crowd cheered. They chanted, "Potassa, Potassa, Potassa." She rode away down toward the beach. She was such an acid trip.

That evening at a harbor-side table, I observed a number of celebrities motoring in and out of the harbor on their yachts, or just strolling along the water. I noticed a twenty-five foot bright yellow cigarette boat with red racing stripes pulling up to the dock. Two muscle-bound body builders in Speedo bathing suits lifted their big, powerful arms to place a dark-haired exotic-looking chick gracefully onto the dock. She wore a suede loincloth bikini and looked like Jane from Tarzan. I turned to a man next to me.

"That's Diane Von Furstenburg. Her ex-husband has a house here somewhere in The Pines."

Late Sunday night, I caught the last ferry back to the city. My head spun with the events of the weekend. Now I knew I had two things to live for—The Saint in the winter and Fire Island in the summer! As I got off the ferry at Sayville, a big black stretch limo pulled up to the boat. I saw a tall, dark-haired figure step from the limo. It was Dwain just arriving. I couldn't believe it. *How does he always do that?*

Without the ball and chain of the Evil Stepsisters my appetite for partying was insatiable. Every Saturday night for the rest of the summer, I took the train to Sayville, then the boat to Cherry Grove or The Pines. I hid my overnight bag under the boardwalk and danced all night, tripping on MDA at the Ice Palace. In the morning, I grabbed my bag, had some breakfast and used the restaurant bathroom to wash up, brush my teeth and change into a bathing suit. I spent the day at the beach, and then washed up for the Sunday tea dance in The Pines, always keeping my bag hidden under the boardwalk so no one would know I was a day-tripper. Late Sunday, I took the boat and the train back to New York. It wasn't a restful weekend, but it was so much fun.

Autumn came and I became a regular at The Saint again. I was still doing a bag of pharmaceuticals every weekend, but fooled myself into thinking it was okay because I stayed straight throughout the week. I was getting pretty good at cutting hair and networking. The next summer, I cashed the Israeli bond that Fanny had given me for my Bar Mitzvah. I answered an ad for a share in a pool-house on Fire Island. The men who lived there wanted to interview me to make sure I was acceptable. There were five of them: two older models, Yolpe and Bryce; a talent agent named Gary; Carl, the man who actually interviewed me; and his lover, Ralph, who ran the house. It was very expensive and I could only afford every other weekend. Ralph was about fifty. He was a tall, dark, handsome Italian and he always wore tight pants to show off his huge cock. His spoke with a Brooklyn accent with a slightly sarcastic edge. He gave the impression that he had seen and done it all. He saw through all the bullshit in people. When he began to like me I felt honored, because he didn't like everyone.

Carl was a forty-something from North Carolina. He had light brown hair and eyes and an incredible body. He was always talking about reincarnation and stuff. Ralph and Carl had been lovers for fifteen years. Their relationship was open. Sex with other people was okay as long as it didn't get romantic and they did groups. In retrospect, I think they were probably sex addicts, but I didn't know anything about that at the time, nor did anyone else. They taught me a lot about how I should act, but mostly, they made me feel accepted. They were always pointing out when people were attracted to me. Because I was young and clueless, they eventually became like parents to me.

Ralph would often sit on his deck watching the people go by and give me the inside scoop on all the celebrities. I saw Jerry Herman and Carol Channing, Kay Ballard, Liz Taylor with her husband, Senator John Warner, Tommy Tune, Claudette Colbert, Roy Cohn and Cher. The most notorious was the threesome of Egon Von Furstenburg, Calvin Klein and Steve Rubell. They were always looking to procure young boys for orgies at Calvin Klein's beautiful beachfront home at the end of Driftwood Walk.

Egon Von Furstenburg approached me one night. His house manager grabbed me by the arm, rendering me captive, while Egon leaned over saying "My name is Egon—Egon Von Furstenburg. I'm in the book on East 33rd. Call me. I have a big dick." It freaked me out while I was tripping, but I was learning that having a big dick was a hot commodity. I didn't want someone to tell me I was big. I wanted them to tell me I was beautiful. I was still into the gay mating dance and the idea of going home with my future husband. I was extremely shy with men I was attracted to, so I hung out with Dwain at his house, or with Ralph and Carl. I did so many drugs that Ralph and Carl were truly worried about me. When I was really high, I would stay with Dwain until I sobered up for fear of upsetting Ralph and Carl.

BEAUTIFUL DISCO FAG

I met a hairdresser named Raul. He was a stylist who did magazine shoots and he asked me to cut his hair. I suspected that he wanted to fuck me. I also thought he might have some interesting contacts, so I agreed to meet him at his apartment the next evening. I cut his hair. He gazed into the mirror admiringly, then turned around quickly and grabbed my ass. I was taken by surprise so I moved away. He moved closer to me and before I knew it, he was chasing me around the apartment. The chase ended with him pushing me into his bedroom and we fucked. After our rabbit heart rates returned to normal, Raul turned to me. "Mark, I'm sorry, man. I didn't mean for that to happen. My lover, Bruce and I have an open relationship and I'm sure he'd like a three-way with you. If you want, I'll get him to get you a job at Pierre Michel where he works. You know it's the most exclusive salon in New York. If you want to make it, you really need to work on 5th or Madison."

The Pierre Michel Salon called me at my job to set up an interview. It all went well and they told me I could start in a month. They also said I could keep my old clients at the lower prices for a while and charge the new ones the higher prices.

As I walked outside after the interview, there was a bounce in my step and I was humming.

I was still trying to stay sober through the workweek and wasted only on weekends. I didn't do coke unless someone turned me on to it. It was too expensive. The weekend before I was to start my brand new job, I was dancing at The Saint. When I went into the bathroom, a tall guy with curly hair asked me if I wanted to do some coke.

"Sure," I replied.

Suddenly another guy, not as handsome as the first, interrupted, "My coke's better than his." "Why, I'll be the judge of that," I said. His was definitely better. I hung out and danced with him for the rest of the night. He was average looking, about 5'10" with dark hair and eyes, and he was very hyper. His name was Steven Pines.

I wanted to go home by myself. Steven insisted on walking out the door with me. Since I only lived a few blocks from The Saint on St. Marks, I usually walked home. Steven followed me, talking on and on and on about nothing. My friend from Syracuse, Andy, was staying at my apartment for a few days. He was a model and supposedly straight and had a girlfriend back home, but on a few occasions Andy and I ended up in having sex in our sleep after drinking too much. The next day we pretended it didn't happen. He was a very handsome, wholesome-looking guy, with all-American features and a body builder's physique. He tended bar uptown at Manhattan Skyline and modeled swimsuits and underwear. He loved coke.

We approached my door. Steven Pines said, "Please Mark, I just need to use your phone for a minute. I know you have a guest, so I won't bother him."

I lied. "No, my brother is staying with me."

"Come on, Mark, maybe your brother would like some coke. Then I'll make my call and go."

"Okay." At this time in New York, coke was all the rage. Cocaine was God's way of telling people they had too much money. Straight doctors and lawyers were serving it from silver bowls at parties and everyone had their own coke spoon. It was illegal, but socially acceptable. Clients tipped me with coke.

Steven made his phone call and turned Andy and me on to some lines. I finally pushed him out the door and went to sleep. At about 5:00 am the next morning the doorbell rang. I was expecting someone from out of town—a guy I really dug. His name was Bill, a Tommy Lee Jones look-a-like from Austin, Texas. He was coming to town for New Year's Eve and wanted me to take him to The Saint for their huge, members only New Year's Eve Party. I had sex with him once, but wanted more, so I hurried to the bathroom to brush my teeth and fix my hair. I went to open the door.

"Mark, please, I'm sorry to bother you. I just need to use the phone quickly." Steven Pines pushed into the apartment and started piling coke all over my glass coffee table. I started to panic. I was afraid of how this would look if Bill showed up and I was afraid my cat Ginger would eat the coke and overdose and die. Still, I hated to turn down free coke. My friends would die for this much coke. I had never seen so much coke. There had to be at least one thousand dollars worth of it on my coffee table. I got some plates from the kitchen and covered up the piles of coke so the cat wouldn't eat it. "Listen, Steve, you have to leave right now. You're ruining my life, you asshole. You'll have to get the fuck out—now!"

"Okay, Mark, don't get so upset, I'm so sorry. I really didn't mean to upset you. Just take my card—if you ever need anything, just call me. I promise I won't bother you again."

I looked at the card. It said "Steve Pines, Fine Clothing, Pirates of Penzance." The coke remained in piles under the plates. About an hour later, Bill showed up. I told him what had happened, then picked up the plates and showed him. After inhaling several lines, Bill said, "God, you should have let the guy stay, man."

Bill and I left to get the New Year's tickets at The Saint. I told Bill all about my new job at Pierre Michel and how I was going to make all this money and all the famous people's hair I would probably do. I must have rubbed him the wrong way with my materialistic and status conscious ways. Bill went with me to the Saint that night, but towards the end of the night, he said, "You know, you think you're so cool, talking about your job and all the money you'll be making. I bet you think you can get whatever and whoever you want. You're a spoiled brat;—I'll see you later, man."

When the world doesn't confirm your existence, you take confirmation wherever you can get it. I took mine at the salon. One good thing about coke is that it numbs your emotions. You can't feel the hurt. I turned and went back to the dance floor thinking about the next hot-looking man and how I was going to be rich.

A few weeks later, I was at Mark M.'s apartment with Milton and Phil. Everyone was calling around looking for coke, but no one in town seemed to have any. I pulled Steve's card from my wallet and said, "I think I know a guy who might have some." I regretted it even before the words left my mouth, but I dialed the number.

Steve said, "Hello.

"Hi, Steve, it's Mark from the Saint."

"Mark, I am so glad you called. I'll be happy to help you out. Meet me tonight at this mansion, The Rutherford House on 14th Street. There's a party tonight for the group Adam and the Ants. Your name will be at the door."

The cab arrived at the shabby old mansion. You could tell it had been elegant once.

"Mark, come on in. I'll show you around. Don't you think this place is groovy? It was really something grand at one time. The owners rent it out for parties to rock groups."

He walked me up an old mahogany staircase to the second floor. There were all kinds of really punked out characters milling about. The smoke was thick and punk rock blasted from speakers. As we continued up to the third floor, I noticed that all of the small bedrooms had what looked like Puerto Rican hustlers standing in the doorways. I thought it must be some kind of male brothel.

"Uh, Steve, I really don't know if I'm going to be able to hang out here very long."

"Oh, okay, I'll tell you what. You tell me what you need for your friends, and I'll drop it off when you want to go. I have a driver and a limo waiting downstairs. He'll take us anywhere you want to go. Listen, I don't know if I told you, but I've got a really cool clothing store I own in SoHo called Pirates of Penzance. The clothes are really hip. I'll take you to drop off the coke to your friends and we'll go to my store. You can pick out anything you want. I know you'll like the clothes. No strings attached."

I loved hot clothes.

We got into his limo and delivered the coke to Mark M. and Milton. They were in shock that I delivered Grade A coke in a stretch. Steve and I went to his store in SoHo.

He let me try on whatever I wanted. He sat on the couch in front of the mirror snorting more lines. It seemed like he had a never-ending supply. He talked incessantly about the parties he went to and the businesses he owned. He seemed incredibly intelligent, but there was something disturbing just beneath the surface. He let me keep a shirt and two pairs of really nice pants and we locked up and left. Surprisingly, he took me home and didn't pressure me to let him come up.

The next day was Monday. I went to bed at midnight so I'd be rested for work the next day. At 5:00 am, Tuesday morning, the phone rang. It was Steven. The punk music was blaring in the background.

"Mark, baby, come out and party with me. I'll pick you up in the limo, man. How about it, dude?"

I might have been a disco party boy, but I worked really hard during the week and now that I had a really good job, I didn't want to fuck it up. "Look, Steve, I'm not into this. I have to go to work in a few hours. You can't fucking call me at these late hours. I don't want to come out and party," I said.

"Okay, Mark, now I can tell you're angry with me, man. Don't get mad—I was just sitting here thinking of you, wishing you were here, that's all. I won't bother you again. Go back to sleep. I promise not to bother you again." He seemed remorseful enough. I hoped what he was saying was true.

He called again the next night and the night after that at 4:00 and 5:00 am. This guy never went to sleep. The third night I really lost it. I couldn't get a good night's sleep and I was afraid of screwing up my new job.

"Look Steven, I'm telling you right now, you fucking scum bag. I don't want anything to do with you. You're making me a nervous wreck. I can't get a good night's sleep for fear of your fucking insane late night phone calls. I want you out of my life. Do you hear? I want you to come and get these fucking clothes you gave me. I don't want your fucking coke, your fucking clothes or your fucking limo—nothing, especially you! Asshole!"

I had no intention of sleeping with him.

"All right, I promise never to bother you again."

The doorbell rang. I was in a robe and slippers. It was 4:00 am and I had to get up for work in a couple of hours. I went downstairs with the clothes in a bag. I was just going to hand him the bag and go back upstairs to bed. There outside my building was Steven's big black limo. The door opened and a hand reached out. I started to hand him the bag, when the hand grabbed my wrist and pulled me into the back of the limo. The car sped off before I knew what was happening. Steven was sitting in the seat opposite me with two other guys. They were obviously wasted on coke.

I was totally losing it. I was really angry, but afraid. "Steven, you fucking asshole, I want to go home, now. I told you I don't want to go with you—anywhere. You can't take me in this car against my will. This is kidnapping."

Steven and his two pals started to laugh.

"Oh, Mark, calm down, man—you're acting like a little girl. Here, do a few lines—we'll bring you home in a little while."

"I don't want to do any coke! I want to go home to sleep and go to work in the morning. You can't just take me against my will."

I felt violated. I wanted out, but they wouldn't listen. The limo drove all around The Village up to 23rd Street to the Chelsea Hotel. Steven and his two goons got out to do some kind of coke deal or something.

I had no money, no shirt, no coat, no shoes and it was snowing heavily. The situation was overwhelming. I started to cry. The driver heard me, but said nothing. When Steven got back into the car, the other two men weren't with him. He started going on and on about how sorry he was, but he just wanted to be with me. He was much too high to notice the direction we were going. I wouldn't talk to him.

The driver headed down Second Avenue and back up First. He stopped at my corner on St. Mark's Place and 1st Avenue and said, "Get out of here. I don't want anything to do with no kidnapping."

I opened the door and jumped out. I ran home in my robe and slippers, in the freezing cold air with two inches of snow on the ground. I ran upstairs and locked the door. Every night for weeks he called in the middle of the night. When I heard his voice, I hung up. Twice, I looked out my window right after I hung up and saw his limo speed away down the street. I wasn't getting much sleep and I was getting extremely paranoid. I decided to get an answering machine. I wanted to stay listed and I didn't want to change my phone number because I had just started my new job and wanted my clients to be able to find me. So, I left the answering machine on and turned off the ringer on the phones. Late one night a friend named Juan called.

Beep. "Hi, Mark, it's Juan. I'm down at Studio 54 with Dom and Rico. We want you to come and party with us." Click.

"Thanks Juan, but I'm tired and I'm not into it—thanks anyway."

"Well, hold on a minute, because someone here wants to talk to you."

He put Steven Pines on the line. "Hi, Mark."

"Drop dead, you sick motherfucker," I screamed. I slammed the phone down and paced the floors of my apartment. I was losing my mind. I just wanted to cut hair. That was the whole reason I had a phone.

I got a strange call from the owner of the Odeon Restaurant in SoHo, a very trendy restaurant that was difficult to get a reservation. "Hello, is this Mark Okun? This is Brian McNally, the owner of the Odeon on Varick. We'd like to have you come to the restaurant for dinner tonight as our guest."

"But, I don't even know you. Why would you invite me for dinner?"

"Well, a Mr. Steven Pines is here and asked me to request the pleasure of your company."

"Tell that fucking asshole to drop dead!" I yelled. I knew he was getting all these people coked up so they'd call me. It was amazing what people would do for a line of cocaine.

The 4:00 and 5:00 am calls continued, despite my steadfast rebukes of his favors and attentions. Even though the machine was answering, I could still hear his increasingly disturbing messages in my small apartment. I couldn't sleep. I was late for work. I was so paranoid, that before I'd leave my apartment or come home at night, I'd ask my neighbor to check outside for limos. I was being stalked and was getting fearful of my life.

My friend and sometime brother, Andy, who was still staying with me said, "Mark, you're letting this guy ruin your life. It's affecting your job. You're afraid to go out. You've got to take control of the situation."

The next day at work, I was late again. My boss was really pissed. "All your partying is taking its toll on you, Okun. You're always late and you look like shit."

"It's not partying. I'm being stalked by this guy." I told him the whole story as he was cutting a client's hair. The man in the chair listened intently to every word. After I finished, the client turned to me and asked, "Excuse me, but what's his name?" "Steven Pines," I said. He continued. "He's telling the truth. I'm the guy's lawyer. Steve's crazy, but he's harmless. He was a famous photographer and made a fortune, shooting all the rock stars in the early seventies. Then, he went off the deep end. His roommate was the one who fell off the bridge at Studio 54 and died. Just keep ignoring him. Eventually, he'll leave you alone."

That weekend, I decided I wasn't going to let this guy put me in prison. I wanted to go dancing at The Saint, so I went. I was having a great time. I had taken some MDA. I walked up the stairs to the balcony for a break after dancing. As I was gazing down at the dancers, I looked around. There below me was Steven Pines. Of course, he saw me too. He started screaming crazy shit and ripping off his clothes. White foam oozed from the corners of his mouth and his bloodshot eyes nearly burst from their sockets. I ran down the stairs looking for the manager. "You've got to help me—this crazy guy is freaking out. His name is Steven Pines and he's been stalking me for months."

Steven was running through the dome in only his underwear screaming, "I'm going to kill you, you beautiful disco fag."

"Hide in the D.J. booth. If he sees you, he'll just get more upset," said the manager, Jack Stoddard.

"What did you do to him?" asked Sharon White, the DJ.

"Nothing—I never even slept with him."

I watched from the DJ booth as five bouncers carried him kicking and screaming, gathering up his clothes and trying to get them back on him. This guy sure didn't look harmless, as his lawyer said. He was certifiably nuts. The Saint had a policy of getting people they thought were overdosing out the door as soon as possible, so they wouldn't be held liable for insurance reasons.

My friends thought the whole thing was a joke, especially Mark M.

"Poor baby. I wish someone would kidnap me in a limo and shove coke up my nose."

Steven's calls continued through the next week. One night he managed to get into my building. It was 3:00 am and he started banging on my door. I pretended not to hear him and curled up in my bed with pillows over my ears. Finally, the knocking stopped. I got up to get a glass of water. There was a note slid under my door. It read, "I'm going to kill you, you beautiful disco fag."

Now, I had evidence and I decided to go to the police. I had saved all the tapes from the answering machine for evidence in my murder trial. I was convinced he was going to kill me. I waited about half an hour after he left and went straight to the police station.

My prior experiences in Syracuse as a juvenile didn't leave me with a positive impression. I always felt like the police were on everyone else's side, not mine. I tried to tell the story as calmly as possible. I knew the macho cops were going to listen to me, look me over and think that I was just another hysterical fag. There were two male cops and a nice black female cop. The first cop, a burly veteran of the force, told me I had to go downtown to obtain an Order of Protection. Until then, they could do nothing. The female cop seemed a lot more sympathetic. She told me she could tell I was really scared. She gave me a cup of coffee and told me to sit down until I calmed down. Once I regained my composure, I gathered up all my evidence and told the lady cop I was leaving.

I laid low for the next couple of weeks. The calls slowed down and I was beginning to hope that he was finally letting up. Three weeks later, I came home around 5:00 pm As I was listening to my messages on the answering machine, I heard the voice. It was Steven and the message was for Andy!

"Andy, hi, Steve here, I'll pick you up in the limo at 11:00 for brunch at the St. Moritz. Looking forward to it. See you then."

How could Andy go with this deranged asshole after all I'd been through, and after he lectured me about staying away from him because he was ruining my life? Now, I was worried. Andy wasn't home. I watched and waited. I was convinced that I would never see Andy again. The sound of my doorbell snapped me out of my state. Not taking any chances, I asked over the intercom who was there. It was Andy and when he got to the door he looked terrible.

"What happened to you? Are you all right? Are you hurt?"

Andy's shirt was torn at the collar and the sleeve. His mouth was swollen and bleeding; he reeked of alcohol. Andy sat down. "Steven picked me up in the limo. We went to the St. Moritz Hotel and started drinking. He ordered brunch and we ate and drank some more. When Steve went to the bathroom, the maitre d' came over to me and said you look like a nice boy, so I think you should leave now. He said Steve had run up a huge tab over the month in the hotel that he couldn't pay. He said the police were on their way to arrest him and it would be best to leave before they got there. By this time, I was drunk and high and I had no money for a cab, so I had to walk home.

"Somewhere around 23rd Street, two big Spanish guys with black leather jackets and chains all over them asked me for my money. I told them I didn't have any. The bigger one shoved a gun in my ribs and told me to empty my pockets. I didn't have anything in my pockets, except some matches and about a half a gram of coke wrapped in a torn magazine page. They didn't even take that because they thought it was trash. The smaller guy held my arms and the big guy punched me about seven times until I collapsed on the ground. Then they both kicked me and ran away. I just lay there for about a half hour. No one helped me."

I got Andy some ice and a warm washcloth with soap to clean off his face. "How could you have gone with him, Andy, after all you saw him do to me?"

"Well, he sounded so normal on the phone."

But, I knew why he went—it was the coke.

The calls stopped after that. The next time I saw his lawyer at the salon, he told me that Steve was admitted to a psychiatric hospital near his parents' home in Westchester.

MY OLD FRIEND GEORGE MAGILL had a part in "Camelot" at the Burt Reynolds Theater in Florida. He told me I could come and stay with him. It was good to get away from New York for a few days and soak up some warm sunshine. New York was beginning to feel like an insane asylum. George looked good and seemed to be doing well. I told him all about Steven Pines and the kidnapping. We spent the next three days at the theater and hanging out with the cast. George took me to the airport that Saturday morning and I flew home to New York. On the plane, I was thinking of the date I had that evening with a conservative WASPY, nice-looking banker named Tim. He wasn't the kind of guy I was used to going out with, but I felt I needed a break from the Nazi party boys.

Arriving at La Guardia, I flagged down a cab to go home. I didn't even really notice the cab driver; I was so lost in thought, I hopped in. The first couple of minutes we drove in silence. Then, I started to smell something funny, like something burning.

Flames and smoke started to fill the cab's interior. I was just about to jump out of the moving cab when the driver pulled over, reached underneath his seat and doused the flames with a small portable fire extinguisher.

My eyes were burning and through the coughing and choking. "What the fuck happened?"

The driver answered, "I guess the light over my license caught on fire. Are you all right?"

"Yeah, I guess so. Should I get out and grab another cab?"

"Did anyone ever tell you that you have beautiful blue eyes? Do you realize we almost died together? Do you want to get high?"

He pulled out a tackle box of every kind of pill you could imagine; bags of what looked like coke and heroin. I couldn't believe it. I couldn't get away from it all. I felt like the world had gone crazy, at least New York.

Working at Pierre Michel was just the thing I needed to regain perspective after my stalking ordeal. Located a 6 West 57th Street, near Tiffany and Bulgari, it is one of the most expensive corners of real estate in the world. Pierre Michel was a salon for wealthy, upscale socialites and movie stars. There were no scruffy, long-haired potheads here. I thought perhaps I'd found a safe haven from the downtown sleaze, but everyone there was on coke or some other drug. I really wanted to do well, to establish a reputation in the circles where it mattered—this was my chance to really have a career, not just a job. I made friends with the colorist, George Milton, who was very talented. The manicurists were mostly Russian. They liked me so they sent me their clients.

The top hairdresser at Pierre Michel was named Steven Jacobs. He had a reputation for being "on the cutting edge" and was always being written about in fashion magazines. He was one of the first gay men I knew personally who were sick with what the press then called "the Gay Cancer". It upset me deeply to see such a talented man so sickly and thin, with purple lesions on his face. He was so weak that his two assistants had to do most of his work for him. I worried that this illness might affect me because some people were beginning to believe that the drug-infused, gay lifestyle that was so prevalent in the New York and San Francisco fast lanes that I was a part of were the cause of the disease.

My roommate Andy announced that he was going to marry Diane, his Italian girlfriend from home, at the Hotel Syracuse. I didn't have much faith in the length of the marriage, but I was happy for them anyway. He asked me to be his best man. I said "yes". There were about two hundred and fifty people at the wedding. Her father owned a big hardware store in Syracuse. I was a little awkward around Diane and her family. I felt like they could see right through me, that they knew that Andy and I had sex. Andy and Diane looked magnificent at the wedding, especially Andy, and the reception was a lot of fun. The partying went on throughout the weekend and Andy, all his friends and I stayed drunk and stoned for days.

It had been over two months since I heard that Steven Pines went to the mental hospital. My job was going well. Since I was making more money, I hired a cleaning woman. One day the doorbell rang and I thought it was Dora, the cleaning lady. I buzzed her in. When I opened the door, there stood someone I had completely forgotten about. It was Steven Pines with a clean-cut guy I had never seen before. I freaked.

"Steven, what the fuck are you doing here? I thought you were finally in a hospital where you belong. You know I can't let you in."

His companion replied, "Listen, Mark. I'm Allen Sarkin. I'm a friend of Steve's from high school. I've known him all my life and I knew all about his problems. Somehow he managed to check himself out of the hospital. He came to my apartment and begged me to take him to you. He knows he's got to go back. I was trying to convince him of that, when he promised he'd go back if he could see just see you."

I stared at Steven. He looked awful. He'd gained weight; his hair was a lot thinner and he had big black circles under his eyes. He looked drugged, but not on coke.

"Listen." Allen said, "Let him try to get his mother on the phone and let him know we're bringing him back to the hospital."

I let them use the phone. The door buzzer sounded again and this time it was Dora. She came in and I introduced her to everyone in the room. She was walking around cleaning up as the conversation in the living room continued. Finally, after Steven talked to his mother. He and Allen left. I now realized I had nothing left to be scared about, that Steven couldn't hurt me anymore.

I told Dora I was worried about what she'd thought. "Don't worry, child. I used to work at Bellevue, honey, cleaning. I'm used to working around crazy people. They don't bother me none."

Months later, while working at Pierre Michel, I recognized one of the clients sitting in the chair getting his haircut. "Aren't you Steven Pines' lawyer?"

"Ya."

"I'm Mark. I was the guy Steven was stalking."

"Yes, of course, I remember you."

"Whatever happened to him?"

"He was in the mental hospital near his parents' home. Somehow he found out that his parents were in Europe. He managed to get out of the hospital and break into their house. He set the house on fire and he burned to death."

SPIRALING

Sylvia visited me every other month in New York City and it was always fun to be with her. When she came, I tried to take her out to nice restaurants or to the theater. I knew she didn't get out much at home. She let me know that she loved every moment of the time she spent with me in New York and it gave me so much pleasure to pamper her.

I took her to the play *Torch Song Trilogy*, with Harvey Fierstein and Estelle Getty. Sylvia was a big fan of the "Golden Girls" on TV. Estelle played the mother of Bea Arthur's character on the show, so Sylvia was interested in seeing her live on Broadway. The story was about a middle-aged Jewish gay man's mother coming to terms with his homosexuality and their relationship. Estelle Getty played a typical New York Jewish mother. Her mannerisms and one-lines could have easily been Sylvia's. I looked over at Sylvia often during the play to see if she was identifying with the characters. Occasionally, I'd poke her in the ribs and she'd reply, "I get it."

We went backstage to meet Estelle Getty. My housemate from Fire Island, Gary Hochberg, was her agent. Sylvia was thrilled. I thought she'd never stop talking about it. That same weekend I took her to see the musical, *Starlight Express*. George Magill was in it, so we also went backstage. My mom thought I had a very glamorous life and I could tell she was feeling proud of me. I knew she'd have plenty to talk about with her friends when she returned home. I hugged her goodbye as she got in the cab to the train station. She felt small and frail.

I walked to a neighborhood bar. I was sitting at the bar, having a drink, when I looked up to see the most beautiful man I've ever seen. He was looking at me with big black eyes that were surrounded by long curled lashes. His black, shiny hair glistened as he walked over to introduce himself.

"My name is Jesse and I'm visiting here from Brazil." His family had a pied-a-terre in Beekman Towers on Sutton and that they stayed there when they were in the city. "I love New York. New York is freedom. It's a place where you can behave as you wish, do what you want. In my country, because of my family's position, everything is predestined. My life was arranged for me when I was still a baby. I cannot be who I really am or do what I want in Brazil."

I stared into his beautiful black eyes. I knew what he was saying, but I saw it in a different way. I've always pursued freedom in my life, but I would never let my family stand in my way. It wasn't like I was ever going to be disinherited. I was an only child, and there wasn't that much money anyway.

Jesse intrigued me. He confided in me. I felt like he wanted me to know the real him. We left the bar and went back to my apartment. Jesse told me how he'd just lost his father to cancer. Thoughts of Abe and his sudden death drifted through me as I listened to Jesse.

"I have a very close family. My father was the one who controlled it all. When my father became sick with cancer, he wanted only me to be around him. I sat by his bedside and listened to his stories. He told me how he wanted me to see to things after he was gone. The burden on my shoulders was almost unbearable, but I accepted it with honor. I cared for him, night and day, until his death. I knew my mother was hurt, that I, not she, was at his bedside when he died."

Jesse kissed me hard. I felt his pain. I couldn't believe that someone so beautiful would find me beautiful. As we began to make love, I was afraid of the feelings I was having. We fell asleep in each other's arms.

When I awoke, Jesse was gone. My heart sank. I knew it was too good to be true. I got up and made some coffee. The phone rang. It was Jesse. He said, "Mark, baby, good morning. I'm sorry I had to leave you in the middle of the night, but my family worries if I don't come home. They fear kidnapping and the terrible things that take place in New York to Brazilians."

I was glad to hear from him, but I thought this is just too good to be true. What was the catch? They must be really wealthy if they're worried about kidnappings.

He came to see me at Pierre Michel. As I was cutting my client's hair, he came up behind me. His image in the mirror took my breath away. He was so gorgeous my woman client was drooling over him. On my break, we snuck upstairs into a dark hallway of the salon. We started making out and he told me he wanted me inside him later. He asked if I ever came in contact with any other wealthy Brazilian clients. I couldn't think of any and wondered why he asked.

"If you do meet any wealthy Brazilian patrons, please, don't mention my last name. Do you understand?"

That was strange, but I became so excited when he touched me. When we made love, he'd scream out in Portuguese. He appealed to all my senses and at twenty-eight, I thought just perhaps I had found love.

On New Year's Eve, I was going to a party at Ralph's apartment and Jesse would be celebrating with his family at Club A. At 12:05 am. the phone rang at Ralph's. Ralph answered, looked at me, smiled and handed me the phone.

"It's your Brazilian," Ralph whispered.

"Mark, Happy 1982. Want to celebrate with me at The Saint?" said Jesse.

"Yeah, sure." I replied.

"I'll pick you up at your apartment."

I went back home, got ready and waited outside. At 3:00 am., Jesse pulled up in a limo. He was still dressed in his tuxedo and I was in my regular tight jeans and t-shirt. I thought I had never seen anyone more beautiful in my life. I wished those evil stepsisters Mark and Milton could see me now.

We pulled up in front of The Saint. The doorman said the place was sold out. Jesse gave him five hundred dollars in hundred dollar bills and he let us in. We slid into a corner and did some coke and MDA and went out onto the dance floor. We danced really slow and sleazy, with Jesse kissing me and humping me slowly with his hard dick pressed against me.

"Everyone is watching us, Mark. They think we are beautiful. They are jealous of us and what we have." He whispered more into my ear.

We danced until 7:00 am. We walked back to my house enjoying the unusually warm morning air.

"My family is very wealthy, Mark. We own thirty supermarkets in Brazil. Part-time at home, I work for the President, in the capital Brasilia. If you ever meet someone from Brazil, you must never tell anyone that you know me. You can tell your American friends anything you want, but not anyone from Brazil. I feel our souls are meant for each other and I have to continue seeing you. I'll be back in three weeks."

I was totally getting off on the drama of the whole thing.

Later he told me, "I can pay your rent. You don't have to live in such an awful place as you do," he offered.

I felt embarrassed. I never really thought of myself as poor, but I guess compared to him, I was. I was much too proud to allow him to pay my rent though.

"I can't bear it, Mark, but I must go back to Brazil tomorrow."

He walked me to my apartment door, but didn't come up. He kissed me good-bye and I went upstairs. Before his flight left, we spoke on the phone. He was so upset. "Mark, I don't know what to do. I just don't want to go home. I want to stay here with you forever. If I stay, my family will disown me. I will have nothing. What can I do, Mark? Shall I follow my heart? Do you want me to stay here with you?"

I wanted him to stay more than all the coke in Harlem, but I said, "Jesse, you don't know me well enough to throw it all away on me. You need to go home and think about things." I did not want him to lose his inheritance.

Jesse called me from Brazil every other day for three weeks. Phone calls were still expensive then and no one had ever spent that much on me as Jesse had spent on calling me. We'd talk for at least an hour. He was planning to come back to New York City, but not for at least three weeks. He wanted to take me skiing. I told him "I don't want to go skiing," but he said he'd bring his skis anyway.

I was imagining the life we'd have together. My prince had come. The phone rang. It was Sylvia. "Mark, it's Mom, how are you?"

"Oh, Mom, I feel so happy. I met a guy. His name is Jesse. He's young and really rich. He's from Brazil. I think I'm in love. Mom, I've never felt this way before."

"Mark, how old is he, honey?"

"He's about twenty-four. He's so handsome. You wouldn't believe it."

"Mark, you need to find someone older, more established, someone nice, Jewish, like yourself. Someone who'll care for you, not some Brazilian playboy!"

"Mom, I joined the Gay Synagogue here in New York and I go for the holidays, but there doesn't seem to be anyone there that's good-looking enough. They're all nerds."

"Listen to you—good-looking enough—you're twenty-eight years old. I worry about you, Mark. I want to know you're with someone who'll care for you. I won't be around forever. I didn't want to tell you this, but my kidneys are failing. I've got to go on dialysis. They're going to put a shunt in my arm so they can hook me up to the machine."

"Mom, that's terrible. What are we going to do? God—there's so much trouble in the world. I've been starting to worry myself lately. I don't know if you've heard about the gay disease. It's called GRID, Gay-Related Immunodeficiency Disease. I'm afraid it's going around, and I'm not sure why some people I know are getting sick. And sometimes I wonder if I'm going to get it."

"God would never be so cruel as to take my son before me. Please, let me have peace of mind, Mark. And take care of yourself. Go to temple. Find someone who is Jewish. At least they'll know right from wrong."

I needed her approval and I was so afraid to lose her.

Jesse arrived back in New York with skis, looking more gorgeous than ever. The first day here he wanted to go to

Studio 54. I really just wanted to stay home with him. We did some coke and went to Studio 54. I tried not to drink too much or do too many drugs. I didn't want Jesse to see me as an addict or alcoholic, but I was beginning to think I was one. I could party like I wanted when he was back in Brazil. Jesse had a suitcase full of money. There must have been at least ten thousand dollars in it. He went out and bought me an extra television set in case we needed to watch separate programs.

I took him to Manhattan Skyline on the East Side. Andy was bartending. They clicked immediately and the conversation drifted to Andy's wedding and his wife, Diane. I looked at Jesse. His eyes started to tear up and I knew something was wrong. Jesse looked upset. "What's wrong, Jesse—what is it?"

"I have something to tell you, Mark. This is very hard for me...I am like Andy."

I didn't understand. "You're a bartender?"

"I am married!"

"What? To a woman?" I felt like a truck had hit me, but then I thought how unfair and oppressive it was for Jesse that he couldn't be himself in Brazil. That his family and wealth forced him to be what he didn't want to be. I had the *real* Jesse. His wife had the fake one. Instead of feeling angry and betrayed, I thought this could work if he only sleeps with his wife while in Brazil and me in New York, perhaps this would save us both from this new disease, now called GRID. So maybe this wife thing wasn't such a bad idea.

The next night Jesse came to my apartment. He was very upset. "I just ran into my brother uptown. I had told my family I was going skiing in Aspen. I'm not supposed to be in New York."

I understood about the skis now. I also rethought the thing about him paying my rent. "I told my brother I was having an affair with your neighbor, Sherry, upstairs. He could accept this. In Brazil, to have a mistress is accepted. My father had three mistresses simultaneously throughout his marriage. My mother knew about all of them. His mistresses attended my father's funeral. My mother passed out envelopes of money to each woman as my father wished. You've got to help me, Mark. Go get Sherry from upstairs. Tell her she's got to make believe she and I are having an affair."

I went upstairs and got Sherry to take part in this charade. Jesse's brother came by the apartment, but I had to leave. Jesse didn't seem to want me to meet his brother. Whatever she said or showed him took less than five minutes. Jesse's brother seemed to buy the whole thing. No matter how gay you are, it never hurts to keep a curvy brunette in your hip pocket.

The next day the President of Brazil called my house to speak with Jesse. I have no idea what was said because they spoke in Portuguese, but I did know one thing—no president had ever called my house before. I was addicted to the drama of it all. Jesse stayed with me through the weekend. It made me so happy having him to wake up to in the morning and sleep with at night. Jesse wanted to go to The Saint and I was eager to show him off. It felt good to be a couple rather than cruising for a date.

We danced to the sexual beat of the music. As we ere dancing, another guy came up and started dancing with us. Instead of ignoring him, Jesse seemed to be encouraging him to join us. Jesse kept pushing me towards this other guy. Jesse was coercing me into a three-way. The thought of seeing Jesse with someone else was just too much. I thought he loved me and now he wanted someone else. I was not enough. I freaked. "Jesse, I thought you loved me. How could you do this when we have such little time together as it is?"

I grabbed my coat and flew out the door. I grabbed the first cab I saw and looked back to see Jesse right behind me in another cab. We both pulled up in front of my apartment together. "Mark, please. You don't understand the Latin culture. Sex is in our blood. You know I love only you. Sex with someone else could never be anything else. At home in Brazil, we have what we call the Macumba Festival. On New Year's Eve at Copacabana Beach, voodoo worshippers celebrate the pagan gods. For one night each year, everyone goes crazy and has sex with everyone else. It is a wild time but it doesn't mean anything with regard to our relationship. I didn't mean to hurt you, Mark. You can't understand because you're Jewish and I'm Latin."

I didn't understand at all. I wasn't raised like that. I guess I was much more conventional than I thought.

Jesse came in and we slept together that night, but it wasn't the same. My vision of Jesse as my true love was shattered. He returned to Brazil and called me every night telling me over and over how confused he was and how much he loved me. I was confused too. I was beginning to think that I liked him better over the phone.

Jesse came back to New York and stayed with me a few more times. I really loved him, but I couldn't accept his ways. When we broke up, it nearly tore me apart. The last time I saw him, we went to The Saint together. During the night, we got separated and I left, unable to find him. I just assumed he ran off with someone else. I stayed up all night at home doing coke and waiting for him. He never bothered to come home.

I called Sylvia. "Maybe I should just agree to the threesome," I said.

"Your father and I never had these problems," she said.

Jesse kissed and made up one more time after that miserable evening but I knew our relationship wasn't meant to be. My whole world came crashing down. I had never felt so depressed. I wished I'd never met him. I was self-medicating with cocaine and alcohol, drinking and getting high by myself not just to go out. Once I started doing it, I couldn't stop. I'd stay in the house all day, just doing coke. I had no friends around to talk to. Mark M. and Milton had both moved back to Syracuse and our other friend Phil was sick. I was beginning to wonder if I'd get sick too. The weight of my breakup with Jesse, the drugs, and worrying about getting sick were too much for me to handle. I knew I needed help. I asked around and found a therapist.

In therapy, I tried to work out some of my fears. I stopped confiding in my mother, which she was probably grateful for. Her health was never good. She smoked and had been on dialysis for almost a year now. I lived with the constant fear that when she died, I would be truly alone in the world. Sylvia never complained. She continued to work for years while on dialysis. She had a real inner strength.

We tried to work out my obsessive thoughts of Jesse. I worried that I had done something wrong. Maybe I should have done the threesomes. I wondered if he ever really loved me. Did he just lie to me? I was convinced that I was pathologically naïve. My therapist listened, but offered no solutions.

Two of the busiest hairstylists from Pierre Michel, Donald and Suki, were going out on their own. They asked me to work for them, so I quit Pierre Michel and went to work at their chic new salon, Donsuki, in the penthouse in the Crown Building on Fifth Avenue. I welcomed the change of scenery. I was hoping it would be enough to get me to stop obsessing over Jesse. I just couldn't shake the feelings of hopelessness. I was at my new job for almost a week, when I got on the wrong subway to work and walked into my old salon, Pierre Michel. When the elevator doors opened and everyone yelled, "Hello, Mark," my face turned red with embarrassment. I backpedaled, saying I had just come to say "hello" and ran back to the elevator.

Even as my personal life was a mess, my career was never better. People often told me I was the most talented hairstylist at the salon or even in New York. The colorist, Barry, and I became friendly and he sent me many of his clients including Mrs. Nelson Doubleday, and Mary Carpenter, from Peter, Paul and Mary. I started doing an actor from Queens. Mercedes Ruell asked me to be her date for the opening night of *Lost in Yonkers*. I did her hair for the opening night party and again on the night she won the Tony award. I was styling the hair of various minor titled Europeans and celebrities and I was also cutting Sidney Biddle, the Mayflower Madame and others. I thought to myself—this is what I worked so hard to achieve and I don't feel anything. I didn't feel successful at all. I didn't have anyone to share things with. What did it all matter?

I had joined a gay synagogue. Maybe it was time to take mom's advice and find a nice Jewish guy to settle down with. During the Yizkor service, the part of the holiday service where you remember loved ones who have passed away, they announced the names of members who had succumbed to the disease called GRID—more and more people I knew were dying.

I felt as if my life were spiraling out of control. Yet, somehow I managed to make it through. I can only owe this strength to Sylvia and Abe. They raised me to do the right thing—go to work, be honest, be kind, honor my family and treat others the way I wanted to be treated. These basic values kept me afloat, even though I was drowning in alcohol and drugs.

I THINK MANY PEOPLE END up confiding in their hairdresser personal information they would never ordinarily share. One client who I grew to know well as I styled her hair was to become a bright spot in my life. Sophia de la Renta was one of the most beautiful women I'd ever met and probably in the world. She had the fullest, most lavish head of sable brown hair I'd ever seen. I did her hair twice a week and every time I'd blow her hair out, people would ask me to do their hair like hers. It was the tail end of the eighties era of big hair and everyone wanted big full hair. Sophia was very good for business. Every time she walked out I'd get five new clients.

Sophia's father was a scriptwriter to Fellini and her mother was an upper class English redheaded beauty. When she was a child, Sophia was sent to boarding school in France and England. Sophia's father left her mother for her older half-sister resulting in her mother having a nervous breakdown. Her mother deposited Sophia and her brother in a French convent when she was six and she couldn't even speak French. She told me of her feelings of abandonment.

Sophia told me of her passionate, physically affectionate Italian father and her proper English mother who had been married a total of five times. I, in turn, told her of my own adoptive parents and feelings of never really fitting in. We became good friends. Even though our backgrounds were totally different, I felt that fate had brought us together. One day, Sophia was listening to my mishigas about Jesse. She would try to help me gain some perspective. She said in her Audrey Hepburn accent, "Really darling, bars are not the proper place to meet people. You simply must start meeting a better class of people."

Sophia distinguished money from class. In my mind, the two had always been the same.

"Please, darling, for me, give it a try. I can't claim to be an expert in psychology, but I've learned a lot from my own experiences. When I was seventeen, I married a count and we cruised the Mediterranean on a sailboat for a year. I thought it would be rather fabulous to go off and get married. I was tired of school and he offered me freedom and adventure, sailing the Mediterranean, until we tired of one another and moved on. I was only eighteen and already married and divorced. The second time I got married I was looking for kindness and stability. I met my second husband at a family party. He was a Jewish banker from Washington. I cared for him deeply and thought he loved me too."

"What happened to him?"

"I found out he rather liked boys. I really lost it, darling. I left him and all my belongings behind. Perhaps if he had been honest with me from the beginning maybe we could have worked something out."

I told her about Jesse and how I found out that he was married. "What happened when you found out your husband was gay?"

"I wanted nothing more to do with him, darling. It was absolutely horrible. You should be happy that your Jesse is back in Brazil. A situation like that would be intolerable for you, darling."

"If only I could just get him out of my mind."

Sophia and I remained close. She started dating a man named Ted who was a multi-millionaire from California. He had come to New York to build an art museum to house his art collection. The city gave him such a hard time with permits and zoning requirements that he picked himself up and moved back to Beverly Hills. He was infuriated by the fact that he was donating his art collection and providing the city with a museum and they would give him such a hard time. Before he left, however, he and Sophia got married. I did everyone's hair for the wedding. I felt sad about Sophia marrying and moving to California, but was happy for her. I knew that Ted didn't like me very much. It was because Sophia confided in me everything that was between them. As far as he was concerned, I knew too

much. Sophia and I kept in touch over the years and she eventually moved to Palm Beach, where our paths crossed again.

Now Peter Allen was dying. It seemed like every time I turned around, another gay man I knew had either contracted or dying of the disease finally known as Acquired Immune Deficiency Syndrome (AIDS). I thought of Jesse and his tale about the Macumba Festival where everyone had sex with everyone. I knew I was at risk, but I was afraid to get tested, as was everyone at the time.

Fortunately, I still had drugs and alcohol. If I wanted a line of coke, I'd run out and get a gram. After I did coke, I'd need alcohol to even out the jitters. I'd drink and do lines all night long. I rationalized that if I stayed away from the places that were most likely to tempt me, I'd be okay. But that didn't work either. I decided not to take a share in Fire Island that summer. Even though I didn't rent a place, Ralph and Carl always invited me to stay with them as a guest. I knew Ralph disapproved of drugs, so I tried to hide my drug use from him. I stayed at Dwain's house nearby when I was too high to come home to Ralph's. I knew I had a problem, but I didn't know how to stop.

One night that summer, I went to a new disco called The Limelight that had just opened in an old church. I was dancing to the music by myself on the side of the dance floor, when I noticed a nice-looking Latin guy starting at me. He was tall and dark with thick, black hair. He had a beautiful smile and I sensed a kindness about him. He wasn't the perfect, poster-boy type I was used to. He wasn't as buff as my A-list friends and his clothes were not ultra chic. But he was still good looking. He asked me to dance. I wasn't sure if I liked him or not, but I gave him my phone number and he called me the next day.

Luis was Puerto Rican, but he seemed to have an Italian air about him. He was much more intelligent than the party boys I was used to. He went to Columbia University on a full scholarship and was working as an international insurance underwriter for a large insurance company. My friends loved him. I tried to fall in love with Luis, but I was still crazy in love with Jesse. I would compare the two and think that Jesse was much more exotic, good-looking and volatile. I tried to discuss these things with my therapist. He said I needed to be less self-centered and concerned about appearances and more focused on other people and their needs.

I was Luis' first boyfriend. He had broken up with his girlfriend and was just coming out. He wasn't jaded and drugged out like my other friends. Everyone told me how nice he was. I continued to see him at the urging of my therapist and friends, but my obsession with Jesse prevented me from becoming as close to him as I might have been. Luis began going to the gym to get into shape. His self-esteem improved because he was finally accepting himself as a gay man instead of living in denial. He was blossoming as a human being and I was sinking deeper and deeper into addiction.

Sometimes I'd stay out all night long doing drugs with an after-hours crowd of mine. This was a small circle of contacts who weren't satisfied to go home at 2:00 or 3:00 am. They weren't real friends, but other addicts, like me, who would leave the clubs and do drugs until dawn. I'd see Dwain there. I knew he was an addict, too. I thought of Steven Pines and how out-of-control he became, but I still couldn't stop. One morning I drifted in around 6:00 am and Luis finally confronted me. "Where have you been? I was worried about you. What's that white powder under your nose? Who were you out with last night? Have you been fucking someone? How could you do this to me?"

"Luis, man," I said as I wiped my nose and noticed a white streak on the back of my hand. "You just don't get it. I lost track of time. And then I got on the wrong train. And…."

"You are such an asshole, Mark. You know, we could've had a good thing. But you're never here for me and the few times that you are, you're always wasted. Haven't I treated you good? I've even been working out at the gym for you. And you treat me like I'm nothing. You know, other guys have been hitting on me lately and I've been saving myself for you. But you know what? I've had it with you. We're through."

I knew my behavior was out of control and my relationship was falling apart, yet I still continued using.

Luis was right and I was a fool not to understand this. I was devastated when he left me. I couldn't face anybody. I chose to run away from all my feelings. I had recently received a letter from my old boyfriend Tom, from Syracuse, the one whose car doors I had smashed. He was living in L.A. now and wanted me to come and visit him. I got on the plane to L.A. in my usual drugged out state. I had no expectations from this trip; I just needed to get away. When Tom greeted me at the airport, I was shocked to see him. He looked so small and unsophisticated. I had turned into a glamour boy and he had remained the same old nerd.

Later, he said to me "Mark, you look really good, buddy. I've missed you. You know, you were right to smash up my car. The way I behaved that New Year's Eve was unforgivable."

I thought, "What an asshole this guy is." I felt so guilty all these years for doing such a malicious and out-of-control thing and now he's telling me it was okay.

Tom liked coke. We copped an eighth and spent the rest of the weekend polishing it off. My friend George was also living in L.A. now, so we went to visit him. George and I, my handsome friends and glamorous lifestyle wowed Tom.

George introduced me to a pretty brown haired girl named Carly. She was a Mormon from Utah. She seemed really nice and very down to earth—to my surprise, George introduced her as his fiancé! I couldn't believe it. I knew George's looks were fading, but I never thought he'd marry a woman. I guess since he was getting older, he just wanted someone to take care of him or something.

I felt really badly for her. I could tell she was starry-eyed in love with this gorgeous actor. She was very naïve. He was verbally abusive towards her, telling me right in front of her, how terrible her hair was and asking me if I would "fix her up." I didn't give this marriage very long. I gave Carly a new haircut and wished them well, but from that moment on, I lost all respect for George.

THE ONLY WAY TO STAY out of the bars was to go back to Syracuse for the weekend and see Sylvia. If I stayed in New York City, it would be another drunken weekend. Sylvia was very glad to see me. The love I had for my mom only got stronger as her health grew weaker.

"Mark, why didn't you tell me you were going to be here? I'll have to shop for some food; there's nothing in the house and everything is a mess."

"Mom, relax. Do you really think I care? I'll get you whatever you need."

"I don't know how much time we'll have to spend together. I have my dialysis appointment tomorrow. My health care worker, Donna, usually takes me to the dialysis unit."

"I'll take you, Mom. Tell Donna to take the day off."

"Are you sure? It's awfully long and boring. It takes close to five hours to complete the treatment. You'll be bored, honey."

"It's okay, mom, if I get bored, I'll take a walk and come back."

We left for the dialysis unit early the next morning. I knew she'd been on dialysis for almost three years, but I'd never actually gone with her. For her, it had become routine. She had no anxiety about it. I acted as nonchalant as I could, but when I excused myself for a break, I felt like I was going to cry. Seeing her hooked up to that machine brought out my worst fears of losing her.

I invited Sylvia down to New York the following month for Mother's Day. She arrived on Sunday morning, I picked her up at Grand Central Station. It was early so we decided to have coffee and something to eat. I knew Sylvia loved cheese blintzes, so I took her to B & H Diner, the home of New York's finest cheese blintzes. The place was small and crowded, but we managed to find two available seats near the kitchen, where two older Polish women with babushkas on their heads were busy making the delicious blintzes everyone was eating. Suddenly, a big black caddy pulled up at the curb outside. A huge, strapping, leather-jacketed guy carrying a huge bouquet of two-dozen roses walked into the restaurant and gave them to one of the women making the blintzes. Her eyes lit up and everyone in the restaurant began to applaud.

Sylvia looked at me and said, "If he was such a good son, he wouldn't let his mother work in a dump like this!"

Later that evening, we were going to see *Steel Magnolias and* I told Sophia about it. "Mark darling, that's marvelous. You should take her to the Four Seasons." She offered to send her limo to pick us up. I knew Sylvia would love that.

At the performance I realized what a terrible mistake I had made. The girl in the play was dying of kidney failure. I looked over at Sylvia so small and frail. Tears were in the corner of her eyes and her hands were shaking. I put my arms around her. "I'm so sorry, mom. I didn't know what the play was about."

"It's all right, dear, I'll be fine. I'm just a little tired, that's all. I think I'd like to go home."

Luis wanted to remain friends. I thought I couldn't handle it, but Luis forced his friendship on me and I'm so glad he did. I also started dating an Italian guy named Rick in Long Beach, Long Island, a friend of George's from California who had moved back to the metro area. He had a great body. Every weekend I poured two hundred dollars worth of coke up my nose. I tried not to drink or do drugs when I was around Rick, but every Sunday night after I left him I would go to the Palladium and drink and do drugs. It was the hot, new club owned by Steve Rubell and Ian Schrager. My old friend Andy was tending bar there now.

One time when Rick and I were at the Palladium, I spotted Jesse from across the room. The sight of him still made my heart race. He walked over slowly and asked, "Hi, is that your new boyfriend? You know I've missed you. I think of you. Are you happy?"

"Yes, are you?"

"No."

Jesse didn't look well to me. I studied his eyes and his body. He looked as if he'd lost weight and he had a tired and sickly look about him. "Are you all right, Jesse? You don't look so good."

"I have been sick with the flu. I'm just starting to feel better. Thank you for your concern. Can we go upstairs and talk? Will you save a dance for me?"

I looked down and thought for a minute. Jesse was a losing proposition however you looked at it. I ran onto the dance floor with Rick. I pulled off Rick's shirt to show Jessie what a great body he had. I danced dirty with Rick. I watched as Jesse walked out looking dejected.

"Who's that, Mark?" asked Rick.

"That's a guy I was in love with. He's a really wealthy Brazilian. Sometimes I think I'll never love anyone as much as him."

"You know, Mark, you are really fucked up. You don't really care about me. All you care about is how much money someone has, how good looking someone is and how much drugs you can do. You play one person against the other, and you don't give a shit about anyone. I've had it." He turned and left.

I walked back to the bar and told Andy to give me another drink.

THE BOTTOM

The AIDS nightmare continued to unfold its horrors. A lot of people I knew were becoming sick, although none of my very close friends as of yet. The gay community talked of little else. It was no longer an elusive illness that couldn't be defined. Now it had a name. People were genuinely concerned about dying. Many people were in denial. If they heard someone was sick, they insisted that they'd never slept with him. Everyone was trying to find a way to differentiate themselves from the people who were diagnosed with AIDS. It seemed as if the most promiscuous men, those who went to the baths and had anonymous sex with multiple partners were becoming sick first. So no one admitted to being promiscuous anymore. They bragged about it before. The worst thing about it was that no one knew about the disease back when they were having unprotected sex. I thought of all the men in the bushes at Fire Island and how any of them could've been a partner of mine after an evening out. The truth was, you didn't have to engage in orgy-like activities. You only had to have sex with one person who had AIDS. You were not only having sex with your partner but with every single person they had ever had sex with. Homophobia was now at an all-time high. Straight people who came to the shop were afraid to have their hair done by gay hairdressers. People were afraid to eat in restaurants for fear that the waiters were infected. I read in a magazine that the Christian Coalition claimed it was God's way of punishing gay people. But that couldn't be true because the lesbians weren't getting the virus at all! Even straight people had become infected. The God I knew wouldn't single anyone out in this way.

Half the people I worked with were sick. My boss, who had worked so hard to build his own business, was now thin and frail. His parents hadn't even known that he was gay. And now that he was dying, it was heartbreaking to see them so full of anger and prejudice. They sold all his belongings while he was still alive. When some friends and I went to see him in the hospital, his mother turned us away. They blamed us for his illness. When he died, they wouldn't even arrange for a memorial service or allow any of his friends to arrange one. His friends and co-workers had one for him anyway. I couldn't believe a mother and father could be so filled with hate.

I was getting paranoid about my own health and after seeing Jesse so pale and thin I wondered seriously if I had been exposed to the virus. One morning when I looked in the mirror and noticed a white film on my throat I decided to have it checked out. My doctor told me to open my mouth and peered inside with a small flashlight. He took a sample of the film on my tongue.

"What do you think it is, doc?"

"It could be thrush, an AIDS-related condition, or it could be nothing."

I looked at the doctor's face. He looked more fearful than I did. I knew, because he was gay and his location was in the city, that many of his patients were gay, sick and dying. It was frightening for everyone in the community. I'm sure he was just as worried for himself as me and it must have been horrible to see all your patients dying and being a doctor yet not able to do anything about it. But I just didn't trust straight doctors. I didn't feel free to tell them everything. I needed to find an AIDS specialist that was up on the new treatments and not as afraid as this guy. Ralph, from Fire Island, would know someone. He knew everyone. Carl answered the phone.

"Mark, Ralph is in the hospital with pneumonia. He's not well."

I had to sit down; I was so upset. This was the first person really close to me who was sick. I tried not to let Carl know how upset I was. "How bad is it, Carl? Is he going to be okay? How long has he been in the hospital? And, why didn't anybody call me?"

"Ralph really wanted to keep it as low key as possible. It's very bad, Mark. Ralph has been diagnosed with AIDS since February."

I was afraid, but I was unconnected to the sadness of it all. I never realized how much I loved Ralph. He was like a surrogate father. Carl must have been worried sick that he'd been exposed. I decided to spend as much time with Ralph as I could. I told Carl I'd visit Ralph in the hospital tomorrow. "Okay, Mark, but please don't let Ralph see the concern on your face."

My doctor called in the morning. The test showed I didn't have thrush. I was so relieved. It gave me a false sense of security. I went to see Ralph in the hospital. I was braced for the worst, so it wasn't as bad as I expected. He'd lost a lot of weight, and he didn't look well, but he also didn't look like he was going to die any minute. I told jokes and talked about all the stuff we did on Fire Island. Ralph was happy to see me.

We made plans for the summer and I agreed to go back to Fire Island so I could be near him. I told him my new-shared house was going to be all Jewish guys and they called it Casa Hadassah.

I tried to put AIDS out of my mind. No matter how hard I tried; I was being sucked deeper and deeper into a fear vortex. I was alone without a lover in a world where it wasn't safe to have sex

Sophia was in New York getting her hair done. She could see something was terribly wrong. "Darling, I don't know what it is since you won't tell me, but I can tell by the way you're acting that it must be life challenging. People face terrible things in their lives. They think they can't handle them, but they do. Miracles happen and things work out." I was sure she had figured out everything, that she knew my secrets.

Ralph's health took a severe turn. By mid-July, he was hospitalized and it looked like he wasn't coming out. His weight was down to one hundred, thirty pounds—this for a man who was 6'3" and usually weighted about two hundred pounds. Carl and I and his sister were the only ones who ever came to see him. Watching Ralph deteriorate day by day ripped a fissure deep in my soul that I thought would never heal. I had never been so intimately close to death before. His bones jutted obtrusively from his body and face. He lost control of his bowels and soiled himself constantly. His skin was covered with the purple sores of Kaposi's Sarcoma. By the time he died, with a Catholic priest administering the last rites as I whispered the Jewish prayer of mourning in Hebrew to myself, I felt I had lived a lifetime. Hell was not pretty and I was only thirty-one.

Ralph's family held a mass for him in a church on Park Avenue with only a handful of mourners. Carl and I went out that night to a disco and drowned our sorrows with alcohol and cocaine, until we couldn't feel the pain. We didn't talk about the loss or the overwhelming fear and sadness that we both felt at my losing a friend and Carl, his lover of seventeen years. I couldn't drink with dinner during the week anymore because I was afraid it would set off a three-day binge. I would just party on the weekends, but my weekend habit was up to three hundred dollars. I was no longer having a good time, and I knew I was an alcoholic and addict.

Someone at The Palladium called me over to say hello. It was Doug, a guy Jesse had known. "Mark, have you heard about Jesse—he's dead from AIDS. His family thinks it was cancer. Even his wife thinks it's cancer."

All the blood rushed from my head.

"Mark, are you all right? Come and sit down. I'll get you a drink."

I covered my face with my hands. Jesse was gone and it was from AIDS. I thought again of the Macumbe Festival in Copacabana. Who else had he infected? His wife? Myself?

I had a friend and neighbor in my building named Greg. He was a body builder / coke dealer. We were friends and I had the key to his apartment in case of an emergency. I had told him not to sell me any more coke because I was trying to quit, but I was desperate. I called him. "Greg, I need something for my cousin who's coming to town. Can you get something for me?"

"Man, who are you kidding? You don't have a cousin."

"How do you know? I have lots of cousins. You might as well sell it to me. I'll just get it from someone else."

I continued on my path to with a single-mindedness that bordered on the pathological. One Saturday night, while hanging out at my home away from home, I saw a nice looking guy I was attracted to across the bar. I tried to get up the courage to talk to him by having a drink first. I was still intimidated, so I had another drink, then another. The alcohol didn't give me any courage; it just made me drunk and then after awhile I just didn't give a shit. I could always go home with a lesser mortal who'd think I was a god.

Greg was out of town and I thought this was good because I would not do any coke, but later that night when I was drunk I remembered that I had the keys to his apartment. I decided to go over and steal a little coke from him and replace it the next day. I went home, got his keys and went to his apartment. I turned the key in the door and opened it. A blood-curdling alarm drove me back out the door. I grabbed the keys, leaving the door unlocked and scrambled to the elevator and back to my apartment. My heart was racing. I threw on my shoes and shirt and ran right back to the night. I drank until my nerves were calm and then copped a gram from the bartender.

The next afternoon, when I could finally lift my head off the pillow and could just about walk, I went back to Greg's apartment to lock the door and make sure everything was okay. Thank God, nothing had been taken during the night.

I had reached an all-time low. I was stealing to support my habit and I would have to admit to Greg what I had done. I remembered the article I had read years ago about Gay AA. I thought I knew it was time. I prayed there would be a nice looking recovering alcoholic there for me. I called information and got the number for AA. I was really nervous and very, very hung over. I dialed the number slowly and deliberately, twice getting an incorrect connection.

Finally, "Hello, Alcoholics Anonymous."

"Umm, uh, I'm looking for a gay AA meeting on the west side, in Chelsea."

"Well, let's see what we have today, Sunday. You just missed the noontime meeting, but I'm sure we have something later. I'll let you talk to Tony. He's more familiar with the gay meetings."

"Hello. My name is Tony."

I couldn't answer.

He continued, "Why don't you meet me at the Holy Apostle Church, on 9th Avenue and 28th Street at 6:00 pm. I'll be wearing a white t-shirt and a jean jacket with a scull and crossbones on it. You don't need to say anything or even talk, but I'd like to see you there." He hung up.

I hadn't said I would, but I felt I had made a commitment to meet this guy, Tony. I had no one else to turn to.

I walked to the address Tony had given to me. It was an old church that had a homeless food kitchen on the first floor and Gay AA on the second. I looked around. The people walking in looked like the most boring down and out people I'd ever seen. I said to myself, "This ain't going to work."

I sat in the back. I wanted to crawl into the woodwork. I wanted to be invisible. I looked around for the guy in a white t-shirt and jean jacket. There were at least four guys who fit that description, each more unsavory looking than the last. Someone came up behind me and tapped me on the shoulder.

"I'm Tony—you must be my caller. Welcome to AA. Make yourself comfortable. I'll be right over there. If you want to sit with me, you can. You don't have to say anything. Just listen." He walked over to the other side of the room and sat down. There were about thirty-five to forty people in the room—all ages, mostly white men, maybe two or three women and a few black people. I was in terrible shape. I was really hung over; my nose was runny and bleeding. I sat there wondering how he knew it was I who called.

The meeting must have started. Everyone went around the room introducing themselves by their first names and announcing their addiction. "I'm Adam and I'm an alcoholic." "I'm Ted and I'm an alcoholic and cocaine addict." "I'm Frank and I'm an alcoholic and over-eater." I thought, oh shit, this is just too hokey to be believed. "My name is Tony. I'm an alcoholic and a drug addict. I was unable to drink even one beer without polishing off the rest of the case. If I smoked a joint, I'd have to smoke the rest of the bag. I couldn't even take an aspirin without taking the whole bottle. I didn't know when to stop, until I ended up in a hospital. I thank God for giving me a second chance. Without all your help, without the strength of the program, I wouldn't be here today."

Instead of being inspired, I was filled with revulsion and disgust. The place was dirty. The people were unkempt and uncool and their haircuts were tacky. I had nothing in common with these people. I was a successful hairdresser with a little drug and alcohol problem. I was nothing like these people. Tony was a low life with bad teeth and bad breath. When he asked me to join them at the coffee shop around the corner after the meeting, I thought I'd die. What if someone saw me with this group? I was afraid people would think I did their hair!

I tried another AA meeting and I even went to a Cocaine Anonymous group, thinking maybe I could just quit coke and still keep on drinking. I went to a meeting and didn't drink or do drugs for three weeks. Since I couldn't go out to the bars without being uncomfortable, I just stayed home. I felt physically better, but I was bored out of my mind.

When one of my clients who considered me to be a family member asked me to do her daughter's hair for her wedding, I did everyone's hair, including the bride's. Everyone looked so beautiful, so full of anticipation and joy. I was caught up in the feeling of euphoria. After the photographer had taken the pre-wedding pictures, the bride asked me to join the rest of the family for a toast before the ceremony. I was nervous because I hadn't drunk in three weeks, but, touched by their gesture of including me in the family, said "yes". The bride proposed the toast and we each had a glass of champagne. The tingle of intoxication hit my brain. I went down to the reception after the ceremony and headed for the bar. I downed beer after beer with shots of schnapps, one, two, three.

The next week I stayed sober throughout the week and went out on the weekend to the bar. I had a couple of drinks and danced and went home. I was convinced I could just be a social drinker. For a couple of weeks, everything was fine. Then I got a phone call from Carl. He had been diagnosed with spinal meningitis and was rushed to the hospital. While he was there, they ran some tests and found him to be HIV positive also. I visited him every day throughout his hospital stay and asked him to stay with me when he got out. I didn't think he should be alone and I needed someone to keep me company.

I started drinking and using coke again after Carl left. The summer was fast approaching and I just wanted to have fun. I told myself if it got really bad, I'd quit everything after the summer and go back to AA. I became boyfriends with a boy who was in one of the most popular houses in The Pines.

Rather than enjoying each other's company and having sex, we spent all our time looking for coke. I was now supporting a $500 a weekend coke habit that I could not afford. On the 4th of July weekend, I got so stoned and drunk that I could hear myself slurring my words and repeating myself. I began to notice the look of disgust in people's eyes. I was disgusted with myself.

The following weekend I stayed in the city, so I wouldn't do drugs. My sinuses were infected from the coke. I took an antihistamine to clear my sinuses and allow me to breathe. It made me feel jittery and high. I felt like I needed a drink. I had some beer I the fridge so I drank all three cans quickly. Now, I felt like I needed some coke. I went to a disco that I didn't even like and paid $20 to get in, just to cop some coke from the bartender. I had to wait an hour for him to take a break. As soon as I got the coke, I ran home and did it all by myself.

I left my house to cruise the docks for sex about 7:00 am. In a fog I grabbed a cab down to 21st Street at the Hudson River. I had heard that people went there for sex after the bars closed. I had never stooped this low before. I looked around at the nearly deserted street and noticed a yellow cab parked nearby. The driver motioned for me to get into the cab. The interior smelled sickly sweet, like strawberry air freshener. The cab driver, smelling of perspiration and barely speaking, signaled to me to get into the front seat where we began sucking each other off. We finished and I walked the six long blocks home. The sun was up and my head was pounding. I hated myself and I hated my life. The Christian Right was right. I deserved to die.

I called in sick to work and slept for two days, which I had never done before. I was determined to change my life, once I felt strong enough to walk out the door. I was physically ill, emotionally barren and spiritually dead. I came to the conclusion that I'd rather be boring and uncool, like the people at the AA meeting, than miserable and fabulous like I am now. I went back to the meetings. I still didn't like the people, but I was determined to stick it out. At the third meeting since my bottom, I was sitting in the dark, musty church listening to 'Joe' share his experiences. He was nothing like me. He was older and dressed shabbily.

He said, "I would sit in my apartment with a small TV going in the background and drink my scotch—it had to be Dewar's White Label. I had no friends. My bottle and my TV were all I had. I'd go down to the liquor store, cash my paycheck and pick up my fifth, then sit and drink it until it was gone. I hated myself, hated my life. I really didn't care if I lived or died."

Up to that point, I'd been comparing myself to Joe, thinking of all the things that made me different and not as bad. I had lots of friends, I hated scotch and I had much more of a life than a small TV and a bottle. But when I got to the part about hating myself and not caring if I lived or died, a light bulb went on in my head. It wasn't about how much money you had, how you looked or what kind of alcohol and drugs you used. It was how the alcohol and drugs made you feel. If, after consuming the drugs and alcohol, you feel empty, alone wanting to die, then you have more than just a little coke and alcohol problem. You are an alcoholic.

The people didn't look as bad to me anymore. I started accepting their invitations to join them for coffee after the meetings. I went to a meeting every day, because I wanted to. I was on a new exciting journey of discovery of who I really was. I told my mother that I was going to AA. She was shocked, but very supportive. She said she should've known a long time ago, because she was always finding me passed out on the carpet in the living room when I was at home.

I actually looked forward to the meetings. They were my new social life, instead of going to bars and drinking. A couple of weeks into my newfound sobriety, I was always running into people who I knew from the bars. I scanned the room looking for interesting or familiar faces. I recognized the platinum blonde hair and chubby face immediately. When she turned to the side, I knew for sure it was my old friend Phyllis. I was very surprised to see her, since we had just done coke together on Fire Island on the Fourth of July.

"Phyllis, how are you doing, girlfriend? How did you end up here?"

"For the same reason you did."

"Aren't you surprised to see me here?"

"No. Even back in our Max's Kansas City days you were the only one they carried in to the parties. Most people just got carried out."

I HAD TO FIND A sponsor, someone who you could call everyday to check in with if you had the urge to drink or do drugs. I picked the name of this guy Ted. He was a short, stocky, Latin guy with sharply defined lines in his cheeks and forehead and the worst hairpiece I had ever seen on a human being. I remembered thinking this was God's way of teaching me to be humble. Ted was a very angry person. He grumbled and muttered about everyone and everything. Unlike before, however, instead of turning my nose up at him, I was determined to make him like me. I called Ted every day. He was patient with me and listened. He turned out to be a great sponsor and human being. One time he came to Donsuki while I was doing a chic client's hair. He wanted to drop off an AA book for me.

There was a look of disdain in the client's eyes. I felt very defensive.

"You don't do his hair, do you?"

"Oh no, but he's a really good friend and a very good person."

Life went on around me. Luis was planning to move to Los Angeles. I had a going-away party for him at my apartment. I knew I had to have alcohol for my guests. It was very scary for me, especially because I had not made any grand announcements about my sobriety, and most people hadn't even noticed that I wasn't drinking. All the guests looked like the Third Reich because Luis only liked blonde guys. I snuck into the kitchen at least three times to call Ted for support. The people in the New York meeting warned me not to go to Fire Island because it was too tempting with all the drugs. But I discovered there were meetings on Fire Island, too. I was so relieved because I always loved the beauty of the beach and the ocean breeze. The meetings on Fire Island turned into my favorite meetings. You could hear the soft soothing rush of the ocean outside the open windows of the building. I would take my small Lhasa Apso dog, Teddy. Teddy went to more AA meetings than any other dog. At the end of the meeting, when everyone held hands and said to keep coming back, "it works if you work it," Teddy would bark.

When I first started with AA, I didn't want anyone to know where I was going. But now, I was developing a sense of pride in my sobriety. I loved the meetings and felt at peace for the first time in my short life. I was thirty-two years old and I finally could see my life clearly. I made new friends on a much deeper level. We discussed our most intimate thoughts and fears. Sometimes, I ran into Dwain. He was always wasted and his striking good looks were beginning to fade. The whites of his eyes were turning the color of the cognac he always drank. I saw him on the boardwalk one sunny afternoon. It was only 1:00 pm, but he'd clearly either already started drinking or had not stopped from the night before.

"Hey, Mark, how are you?" he said. "You're looking great, man, what's going on?"

"Not a lot. Staying out of trouble."

"Is everything okay with you? I mean, you feelin' all right and everything?"

This was becoming a common question these days. Everyone was looking into each other's eyes, hoping to find an answer to the question of whether or not they were sick. "Yeah, I'm fine. I've been going to AA meetings."

"You what?" Dwain started to laugh. "You, Mark? I never thought I'd see you quit drinking." "You should come with me, dude. They have meetings right here in Fire Island, gay meetings with really hot guys. We could go together."

"Fuck you and your little dog, too. No thank you—I love you, man, but forget it."

There was no point in trying to recruit other people to join AA. Desire is the key to agency. They had to want to go. AIDS did not diminish this virtue. In the meetings, a lot of the gay men were sick or dying. I was moved by their stories of their battle with AIDS. No matter what happened, these men wanted to stay sober, so they could live their last days with dignity. It was an amazing thing to watch these men turn their lives around, even with death hovering over them. To me, this was truly the kind of faith I needed to renew my belief in a higher power. These men were proud to be gay.

They knew that AIDS was a disease, not a punishment from God. My heart swelled with gay pride. I saw not only gay men but also lesbians stand up against the homophobia that had permeated society since the AIDS epidemic struck. Lesbians really stood by their gay brothers because the homophobia backlash affected them also, even though they were the group least infected with AIDS. I wondered if I'd have the courage that these people had to find out for myself if I, too, was infected.

An AIDS doctor in the city suggested I begin to get my T-cells counted. An abnormally low count was one of the first indications of infection with the HIV virus, which was the precursor to AIDS. This doctor was very understanding and in tune with the thoughts of a gay man. He didn't insist that I be tested if I wasn't ready to know for sure. The test showed that my T-cell count was 590, in the normal range, but on the low side. I tried to convince myself that I was not infected, but I started to realize that I probably was. I was worried sick all of the time. Sooner or later I was going to have to face the truth. I agonized over whether it was better to know or not to know. I thought of Ralph and Carl and Donald from the salon. I wondered if it would've done them any good at all to be tested before they got sick. There was no one to provide these answers. Even my new doctor, whom I trusted, couldn't promise me anything encouraging if the tests were positive.

When the phone rang these days, I didn't even want to answer it. Dwain's friend Lee confirmed my worst fear. Dwain had Aids related pneumonia and his health was failing. I couldn't bear to think of Dwain, with all his glamour and striking good looks, ending up like Ralph, his body deteriorating before my eyes. My memories of Ralph's death were so fresh that to project the horror onto the Hollywood beauty of Dwain was too much to handle. I followed his progress by phone calls to Lee for about two months. I didn't need a graphic description. I knew what was happening. Dwain didn't want anyone to see him like that. He wouldn't even speak to me on the phone from the hospital. I never spoke to him again after our conversation on Fire Island. Dwain was gone. It seemed like a season of funerals, and the walking dead were left to mourn their passing.

I had to say my final farewells. The funeral was in a large Catholic church on West 16th Street. I remember wishing, if only I had a really good picture of my friend to take away, to remember him by. He was so beautiful. As I arrived at the church, there was a stack of 8" x 10" glossy photos of Dwain as he looked in his prime. I guess I wasn't the only one who felt that way about Dwain's looks. On the back of each picture was a poem written by Walter, Dwain's wealthy, older lover who had kept him over the years. Walter spoke eloquently, extolling Dwain's sense of style and remembering their days in Paris together. Dwain's family sat in the first row. I had met them years ago in my glitter rock days with Harry. They were people of very modest means with not a hint of Dwain's striking good looks. But Dwain was more than a physical beauty; he was a good friend to me. He stood by me when other fair weather friends abandoned me. I thought back to when we were both young and had no money. Whatever little he and I had, we were willing to share with each other.

I thought of losing Jesse, and how it felt to lose someone. For the first time since Jesse and Ralph died, I was sober and alone with my feelings. I felt the pain. Now sober, I cried and cried, and for once, let myself cry it all out. I cried for Dwain's death, I cried for losing Jesse, I cried for Ralph, and I cried for fear of losing my mom. I cried for all the sick and dying people I knew. The plague had truly hit home. This was my holocaust. I couldn't run away anymore. I had to find out if I, too, was HIV positive.

I told my doctor I wanted the test. He explained my options in the event I tested positive. Looking at his face, it was clear to me we both knew what the result would be. Getting the results back and finding out I was HIV positive was in some ways a peaceful revelation. I felt—okay, you're going to die young. In a way, I always felt this was meant to be. My whole life had been in fast forward mode. I never could envision myself as an old man.

I went back to AA every day. My new friends understood the struggle I was experiencing. I trusted them enough to confide my HIV status. I couldn't tell anyone else outside of AA. It could have jeopardized my career. But so could death. There were drugs available for treatment, but most were still experimental. I began seeing a nutritionist who put me on a macrobiotic diet. I lost so much weight. people thought I was dying. I decided to live my life the best that I could until I got sick. I lived it as if any day could be my last. To my surprise, my fear became a small, manageable part of me and I felt free from the burden of not knowing that had become too great. *The truth will set you free, but first it's really going to piss you off.*

SYLVIA

I needed a break from New York. I made arrangements to visit Luis and Sophia in Los Angeles. Sophia, her husband and baby girl Lexa had a drop dead house in Beverly Hills. They lived next door to Elizabeth Montgomery. A redwood forest divided the two properties and the Montgomerys had pet llamas that spit at me when I stood too close to the fence. Luis told me he was dating someone HIV positive. Maybe someone would date me. God, everything is so difficult. I still hadn't told Sophia, but assumed she knew. I was getting over my fear of dying as I woke every morning to find that I wasn't sick. I now had to face my real fear—that I was unlovable to begin with and that I was *damaged* goods. How would I ever find someone to love me? I couldn't imagine anyone who was HIV negative wanting to go out with someone HIV positive. I was afraid to date someone HIV positive, because I was afraid I would end up taking care of a dying man.

The entire gay community was grappling with these issues. Those who were negative were afraid to have sex without asking if their partner had been tested; and those who were positive, were petrified of infecting their partner and also, never being able to find love again. Everything changed again when people began practicing safe sex.

Men, gay and straight, have difficult time talking about sex and keeping their dicks in their pants. By using a condom, you did not have to reveal to your sex partner whether you or he was HIV positive. Gay men never blame each other personally like straights. We knew that no one gave anyone this disease on purpose. We were all infected long before there was enough information to protect ourselves.

I found out from friends that Rick was very sick and so was George. When she learned of George's illness, George's Mormon wife left him, taking their baby daughter with her. I couldn't blame her for leaving. George had a stroke after his wife left and ended up in a nursing home. He called me demanding that I come and see him, but I never did. Rick's new boyfriend stayed with him until the end. George and Rick died within months of each other. I didn't go to either funeral. I couldn't bring myself to attend another funeral. I was sad that they were gone, but I realized I had to save myself for only my very best friends; especially the ones I knew who were becoming sick.

Luis was tested and was negative. I was very relieved. If he had been positive I would have blamed myself. I finally told him I was infected and he accepted my HIV status and was very supportive. I was very concerned about my clients finding out I had HIV. I was afraid they'd leave me, if for no other reason than not wanting to see me get sick and die. I thought when I got sober that my addiction was the only thing that was wrong with me. I was so wrong. I was wounded deeply inside on many levels, and not just from the virus.

the longer I stayed sober, the better I felt. My sponsor, Ted, stood by me through the most difficult and trying times. He used to tell me, "Mark, you think you're a piece of shit, only you think you're the piece of shit the world revolves around."

My own version of the Serenity Prayer became my best friend: God grant me the serenity To accept the things I cannot change, courage to change the things I can, *and the wisdom to know what to wear.*

The most enjoyable part of my life was Fire Island. I thought back to my childhood and the summers on Cazenovia Lake, and it came to me: I longed for a boat. I had always loved my boat as a kid. It gave me a sense of freedom and adventure, and the ocean air would keep me healthy. I was getting too old to share a house with a bunch of guys anyway, but could not afford to buy a beach house of my own.

I started looking around for a cabin cruiser that I could afford and that I could also live on. I owned a large studio coop in a loft building in Chelsea that my mother had given me the down payment for, but boats could be very expensive. I justified the cost by reasoning that if was only going to live a few more years; I might as well do it now while I still could. Sylvia freaked.

"A boat? Are you crazy? How much could you be making, so that you can afford a boat? You have a mortgage and all your other expenses! Suppose the economy is bad and you are not making as much money, as you do now. You should pay off your mortgage first."

"I'll get one big enough to live on, Mom, and that will save me money on a summer share."

"I thought you had grown up by now!"

"I'll name her Sylvia."

"Well, maybe it's not such a bad idea."

I always loved boats since having a small boat and driving my Uncle Phil's bigger boat on Cazenovia Lake as a kid. I took the Coast Guard Power Squadron fifteen week course before I got my cabin cruiser, but I had already taken it once before in Cub Scouts.

The first summer after the Sylvia was christened, I got to know people who were different than I. I enjoyed meeting people who didn't do drugs or drink too much. There was a whole group who lived on their boats and docked them in The Pines Harbor. Most of them were middle-aged Jewish couples. They were called "The Jewish Navy". They stayed on their boats and never took them out. I loved being in the Jewish Navy because it was like being with members of my family in the safety of the harbor. Yet I could still venture out into the wild gay life of Fire Island.

I was close to two couples, the Nowers and the Beckers who lived on 60 foot yachts. Gill Nower taught me a lot about boats and were always fixing everything for me. Felicia, his wife, was always looking out for me. Felicia told me of this boat that I remember seeing that used to dock right in front of the Boatele and was then called the Barbara. It belonged to Barbara Ross of Ross Bicycles and her husband. Barbara looked like a Jewish Dolly Parton. She would sit on her boat decked out in platinum wigs, fake eyelashes, giant diamonds and wave to other passers by on the ferry. She'd hold court on her boat with friends and celebrities during tea and when tea ended they would disembark to dinner in the Boatel.

I wondered why they'd want to dock in a gay town. But Fire Island Pines was a beautiful seaside community. I had to speak Yiddish to get them to believe I was Jewish. I thought the boat would make me seem sexier and more desirable, but most of the guys on Fire Island were too stoned to appreciate it and I didn't want a boyfriend who used drugs. One night I was out dancing at the Pavilion with Ted, my AA sponsor, when I noticed a 4'11", perfectly proportioned, Asian muscle guy moon walking and sliding across the dance floor. A crowed was encouraging him with shouts and applause.

I turned to Ted and said, "God, look at this guy, Ted. Can you believe how he moves?"

"I know. I can't even look at him. All that energy makes me nervous."

"I think he's cute—he's the best dancer I ever saw."

"I think he heard you."

This hot little muscle man danced over to me and wrapped his legs around me and started humping me like a dog, while looking up at me with dark and adoring eyes. I was over a foot and two inches taller than he was. "What are you doing?" I asked

"Let's dance. Come on."

He slinked back onto the dance floor sliding between other dancers' legs and jumping up and down, sliding into a split and twirling in circles. The crowd just loved him. So we boogied like there was no tomorrow. He brought out the John Travolta in me and before I knew it, the crowd was encouraging the two of us on.

The next day I heard Teddy yelp from the top deck of my boat as I was just waking up below. I awoke to find my dance partner standing there with a small bouquet of flowers. His eyes sparkled. "Good morning. Do you remember me from last night? I hope I haven't disturbed you. I found out where you were from your friend, Ed. My name is Duy. I would be very honored if you would join me for dinner tonight."

I had never been asked out in such a respectful way, so I said "Sure." But he was so small, I couldn't decide if I wanted to fuck him or adopt him. We took the boat over to the Grove and docked it in front of a small restaurant. The table overlooked the moonlit Great South Bay. I overheard two queens chatting nearby. One said to her friend, "I heard *her* T-cell count was over five hundred." The other replied, "Personally, I think anyone who has over fifty is tacky."

Duy told me his story of coming to America from Vietnam in 1979. He traveled with his ten brothers and sisters and twenty others in a small boat, leaving his parents behind. His father was a doctor and before the war they were well off. The voyage was frightening but his family couldn't survive any longer in Vietnam. His brother and sisters had a hard time in the beginning, but eventually prospered and were able to send for his parents. He explained, "When I came to Fire Island, I thought I'd found heaven on earth. They don't even have the word that says 'gay' in Vietnamese."

Duy fascinated me. One story led to a thousand stories. We went dancing next and I noticed a drag queen dancing alone in the dark. It was Potassa DeLafayette! Instead of the adoration she had commanded in her heyday, no one seemed to recognize her or even notice her, because all those who knew her were dead.

After we had sex once, Duy and I became friends. The Fourth of July was only two weeks away and we planned to get ready for "The Invasion" together. Every Fourth of July on Fire Island, Cherry Grove invades The Pines. The rivalry between the neighboring towns of Cherry Grove and The Pines has gone on for thirty years. They are both predominantly gay communities. Cherry Grove was usually thought of as a haven for lesbians and older drag queens. The Pines tended to draw a more glamorous male crowd— celebrated artists, muscle men and rich older men and their trophy boys. Cherry Grove was viewed as the tacky stepsister. The Grove residents got tired of being put down all the time.

One day about thirty years ago, close on the Fourth of July, all the Grove residents dressed up in drag, crowded into one big ferry boat and invaded the town of The Pines. Instead of hating it, guys in the Pines loved it. The Pines Homeowners Association asked the Grove if they would do it again the next year. Every year since then, on the Fourth of July, several hundred queens march in every imaginable costume possible at 2:00 in the afternoon off the two ferries singing, "God Bless America." It kind of makes you feel patriotic.

Duy and I entered my boat in the boat-decorating contest. We made a huge red, white and blue sash with the words "Miss Invaded" draped across the boat. We made a giant silver, mylar and rhinestone tiara for the Bimini top; two five-feet tall, high-heeled shoes for the bow; huge red and white, sparkled earrings for both sides of the boat and two huge, fake eyelashes for the windshield. Duy thought up the whole thing and built everything himself. Two thousand people lined the harbor to watch the festivities as they do every year. We won "Most Original." Our friendship was sealed.

I WAS HAVING DIFFICULTIES AT work. The colorist, Barry, was planning to move to a new salon. I had been working with him for the past eight years and he had been referring most of his clientele to me. But, Barry assured me that his new salon would hire me too. The salon business can be very cutthroat, and the new salon never hired me. I'm sure because some evil queen bad-mouthed me to Steven Knoll. Half of my clients started getting their hair done there. The Stephen Knoll Salon was considered the hottest new salon in New York and received a lot of press at that time. I was starting to realize that I would not be able to afford my mortgage and expenses much longer unless I did something. As I was reluctantly getting ready for work one day, contemplating my uncertain future, I got a call that made my immediate worries seem small: Sylvia in the hospital.

"Mark, I don't want you to worry about me now, but I was getting out of the bathtub this morning and I slipped and fell and broke my hip. Uncle Dave drove me to the hospital. They think I'll need a hip replacement."

"Are you in a lot of pain? Is there anyone with you, now? I'll fly up today Mom."

"It's quite painful, but they're giving me medication. No one is here now, but Uncle Dave's coming back later. I think you should wait a while before you come up. I can't spend much time with you while I'm in the hospital and I'll really need your help more after I go home. Then we can spend more time together."

I waited a week, talking to Sylvia every day on the phone. She sounded very weak and I was having difficulty getting any answers from the doctors. I decided to fly to Syracuse anyway. I spent most of the weekend at the hospital with my mother, keeping her company and trying to cheer her up. When I went to visit her late Sunday afternoon before I flew back to the city, I was concerned by her appearance. No one seemed to be monitoring my mother's condition. The halls were deserted. I sat with Sylvia in near silence and she seemed extremely tired.

"Mom, I'm supposed to go back to New York in a few hours. Do you think you'll be okay up here by yourself?"

Her eyelids fluttered open and then closed again. I sensed something was very wrong. Her breathing was strained, and she had never fallen asleep in the middle of a conversation before. She knew I was leaving soon. I tried to wake her but her eyes rolled back in her head. I was starting to panic and called down the hall for a nurse. The nurse on duty was sitting alone behind the desk. She looked up with a bored expression through her half glasses.

"What is it, son, can I help you?"

"It's Sylvia Okun in 243. I think something's terribly wrong."

The nurse slowly lifted her seat and shuffled down the hall. I felt like giving her a good kick in the ass. "She looks like she's sleeping."

"Maybe you should check her out."

Reluctantly, the nurse checked her pulse, opened her eyelids, and checked her blood pressure. The nurse's expression began to change and she became more animated. "Sit with her while I call the doctor."

"What is it? Is she all right?"

The nurse rushed down the hall and soon a doctor and two other nurses were checking her vitals and then began moving her to the ICU. I waited for what seemed like an eternity to speak to the doctor.

"Well, Mark, your mother's in a coma. She's a very sick woman. Fifteen years of dialysis have taken a toll on her body. She's very weak and I'm concerned about her condition. I know it's difficult for you, but the best thing for you to do is to go home and get some rest. We'll see how she's doing tomorrow and hopefully she'll wake up."

"I know she's going to die. No one's watching her. I had to tell the nurse to come and check on her. I can't leave her."

"Mark, there is nothing you can do. We'll take care of her."

I walked to the phone booth and canceled my flight back to New York. Sylvia stayed in a coma all week. I spent the week in her house trying to pay the stack of bills that had accumulated since she first broke her hip. She had good medical coverage, a pension and Social Security benefits that were deposited directly into her account, so there was plenty of money. I visited her twice a day. Finally, Sylvia came out of the coma, but she still had to remain hospitalized. I loved my mother more than anything in world, but I was not prepared to handle the severity of her illness. Even though she'd always been sickly, nothing could prepare me for her decline. The doctors told me I had to make personal decisions to handle what they termed a long-term situation. Sylvia remained in the hospital for five months. She contracted pneumonia on top of everything else and her tiny frame withered to skin and bones. Her hair, previously kept in a warm auburn brown, had reverted to its snow-white color. I brought my scissors to the hospital and kept it neatly trimmed.

I was desperately afraid to leave her, but I couldn't afford to quit my job or even take an extended leave of absence. I worked all week and then flew up on the weekends to care for her. My work situation was a disaster. I was losing clients at an alarming rate partly because of salon politics and partly because in my depressed attitude I don't think was very good company. No one wants to hear about death and dying when they come in for a hundred dollar haircut.

I wasn't exactly entertaining in those days and I had no patience for their petty annoyances and complaints. I was barely making ends meet and I was worried about how the stress would affect my HIV. I sadly wondered who would die first—my mother or I. I wanted her to die first only because I didn't want her to see me sick or dying. She wouldn't have been able to handle it. I had caused her so much pain when I was young. I didn't want to cause her anymore. I couldn't bear to watch her deteriorate. With all the people I knew who died, one hundred and fifty to date, nothing had prepared me for the emotional impact of my mother's death.

The next weekend, I was holding Sylvia's hand about to say 'good-bye' before returning to New York, when her hands began to shake and her tiny body shuddered. Her entire right side seemed to lean over. I ran for the nurse and once again they moved her to the ICU. She'd suffered a stroke. They told me she might not make it. I sat in the waiting room with my head in my hands. I was tortured with conflict. I was afraid to leave her, yet I couldn't afford to miss any more work. I couldn't give my clients any more reason to bolt. I thought to myself, she'd almost died so many times, she might pull through this one, too. She was unconscious and didn't know if I was there or not anyway. I got back on the plane and headed home. I felt that no matter what I did, it was the wrong thing. AA meetings were my only support. I was afraid to discuss things with my other friends because they couldn't handle the terrible unending sadness of it all.

Sylvia recovered from the stroke, but had lost all feeling in her left leg. She'd have to stay in the hospital, probably for another two months and then be released to a nursing home. That would not go over well with Sylvia. She complained bitterly about being in the hospital and I knew I'd never be able to get her to go voluntarily to a nursing home. I got Randy, Uncle Dave's son to help me. When I was at his house he came out with a name and a phone number written on a piece of paper. "I want you to call this lawyer, Mark. He specializes in estate planning. We've got to protect her home and assets. He's going to ask you to go through all her paperwork. Give him what he needs." Randy probably didn't want his wealthy father, my uncle, to pay for everything and have it come out of his inheritance. I didn't blame him.

I called the attorney the next day. Through all my wild antics over the years, even when I was living hand-to-mouth in apartments filled with cockroaches, I always knew that if I were really in trouble, financially or emotionally, I could turn to Abe and Sylvia. I was never completely on my own—without a lifeline to my parents. Now it was I who had to fill the role of caretaker. At thirty-two, I was finally thrust into adulthood.

I dragged out the boxes of bills, canceled checks and important documents, I was told to review. As I was sorting through all the paperwork, I came across one old manila folder tucked in the back of Sylvia's secretary. I found an envelope marked "Mark's Papers." Inside was a yellowed paper with the embossed seal of the State of New York. It read, "The child, Mark Brecht, will now be known as Mark Okun."

I commuted every weekend to Syracuse while trying to keep my own life together at the same time. The hospital told me my mother needed to be in a nursing home. Although she lived through all her childhood illnesses, breast cancer, fifteen years of dialysis, a coma, a stroke and pneumonia, she had reached the point where she was incapable of living independently. I was not looking forward to the inevitable discussion.

"Don't even think of putting me in the Jewish Home. I can't have anyone I know see me like this. I just want to go home."

We found her a nice non-denominational nursing home with gardens and a beauty parlor. It looked like a great place, in which I might even take a week's reprieve from my own miserable existence, but Sylvia hated it. Robert DeNiro's aunt was in the next room and all the nurses got excited when he came to visit her. I took my dog, Teddy, with me to visit Sylvia. All her comrades greeted Teddy and me with their toothless smiles.

"Mark—I'm not kidding, either you get me out of here, or I will arrange it myself. How could this happen to me? I must have been Hitler in my last life."

"Mom, it seems so nice here. The gardens are pretty; the people are polite. It's a hell of a lot better than the hospital. What's so bad about it?"

"You try living here. People scream all night long. Listen, you must find someone to help take care of me and you must bring me home. That is all I ask, Mark. I know I'm going to die soon. I want to die in my own home, with my own couch and my own TV. Please, don't let me spend my last days in this dump. I have a home. We can afford it. Please take me home."

I hugged her tiny body and carefully, I kissed her forehead. "Okay, Mom, somehow, I don't know how, I'll get you home."

There was no going back on my word. I'd made Sylvia a promise and I started investigating our options. On the day that Sylvia was to be released from the nursing home, she was diagnosed with pneumonia and put back in the hospital. This could go on forever. I was so numb to the whole thing. I was sure she was going to die this time. While in the hospital, she was diagnosed with an aneurysm in her aorta. Her doctor explained, "Mark, it's a miracle that she's made it this far—you know that. This complication is much more serious than those she had before. If this aneurysm gets to be one millimeter larger, it will kill her."

"Doctor, she's been dying for fifteen years. She wants to go home. She's begged me. I made a promise to her and I've gotten the house ready for her to come now."

"As a doctor, it's my duty to tell you this woman belongs in a hospital. As a son, if she were my mother, I'd take her home."

We set up a hospital bed in her living room with oxygen tanks with tubes snaking all around the first floor of the house, a commode and a wheelchair. Uncle Dave had a wheelchair ramp built on the side of the house, and we hired a live-in home health care worker to watch over her. I got this woman because she worked for less than if I'd hired an agency. I actually did not know how long Mother would live and I was afraid she would go through all her money and would have none left to leave me. I was sure I had only a year or so until I got sick and I envisioned myself penniless, since my career had also hit the toilet. But the woman was abusive and stole money, so I decided I didn't care how much it cost. My mother deserved to be as comfortable as possible. I cared for her, after all, more than I cared for myself. She was all that mattered to me. Once I hired the agency, things went smoothly for about a month. When I was visiting Sylvia for the weekend, a young nurse's aide was on duty, one of four who tended to my mother around the clock. I had fallen asleep about midnight and Sylvia seemed to be resting comfortably. About 5:00 am, the aide came running up the stairs to my bedroom out of breath. "Your mother can't breathe. I've called the ambulance."

I ran down the stairs to find Sylvia gasping for breath. Her face was nearly gray and I couldn't get her to wake up. I tried talking to her, but I didn't think she could hear me. She looked like a poor dying fish out of water.

"Do you think oxygen will help? What should we do?" The aide was crying hysterically.

"Shut up! I screamed. "Everyone knew this was going to happen sooner or later!"

She stopped crying and started to rub Sylvia's hand and I looked on until the ambulance arrived. I watched as the paramedics worked to try to revive her. They placed a defibrillator on her chest. There were plastic tubes and discarded paper wrappers everywhere littering the living room floor. I felt detached as if I were watching a movie about some other people. I knew in my heart that Sylvia was dead. I tried to sense whether or not she knew she was dying, whether it hurt. I had to know, so maybe I could prepare myself for my own imminent death. It had been ten months since she first broke her hip. I followed the ambulance down Adams Street to Upstate Medical Center. I thought I was thinking clearly. I didn't feel upset at all, until I realized I had just gone through ten red lights.

At the hospital, I sat in a small waiting room. The paramedics told me I could use the phone to call anyone I wanted. This was new. I thought, she must be dead, but she's fooled me before. I couldn't think of anyone to call, anyway. They haven't actually told me she was dead yet.

The doctor walked into the room at 6:35 am. "Mark, your mother is dead. You need to call and make arrangements for her. I'm sorry."

I stared at him as if he were speaking Mandarin. I felt as if the weight of the world had lifted from my shoulders. Watching her suffer for so long had left me completely drained. I was glad it was over. I knew everything would be easier now.

Although I felt exhausted, I couldn't sleep. I called Uncle Dave. He was very upset at losing his baby sister, but in a way, we were all relieved. The funeral arrangements had to be made right away, because the Jewish religion requires burial within twenty-four hours after death, except on the Sabbath. It was a Saturday morning and the funeral was to take place at Birnbaum's on Sunday at 10:00 am. The rabbi gave an eloquent eulogy. There were no family feuds to disrupt the respectful silence. I was moved to hear the rabbi speak of how proud Sylvia was of the boat I had named after her. She used to show pictures of it to friends who came to visit her. I looked around at the people in the room. My family was small now and few of the people who Sylvia cared about were still alive.

I DROVE HOME TO NEW York City, getting a speeding ticket on the way. When I got home around 11:00 pm, I put a disco tape on the stereo. My neighbor, Tom Unger, began pounding on the wall so hard that my collection of antique Art Deco glass shook on the shelves. The walls in the apartment were thin and I guess the bass reverberated through the walls. I usually liked to listen to music before I left for work between 8:30 and 9:00 am, and he'd often bang on the walls and scream. I had complained to the co-op board about his banging before. He was always angry. It was okay for him to blast acid rock all day, as long as it was between 10:00 am and 11:00 pm. I also heard him yelling at his girlfriend and slamming doors. On this night, with my mother just buried, I was in no mood to just sit there. So I banged back hard on the walls in response. I heard him scream, "I'm going to kill you, you fucking faggot." That did it for me. I didn't feel like dying at the hands of some redneck gay basher, so I went out to a bar to hang out with friends.

The next day, Unger was in the hallway as I was walking out to go to work. He grabbed me by the collar. He outweighed me by thirty pounds and his neck was about a size twenty. The veins stuck out on both sides of his forehead and his eyes flashed with rage. While his girlfriend looked on, he brought his face within inches of mine.

"This is between you and me—faggot. I'm sick of your girlie complaints to the Board. If you play that fucking stereo first thing in the morning or late at night again, I'll beat the living shit out of you. You understand?"

His girlfriend seemed frightened by his outburst. "Leave him alone, you're crazy. Leave him alone."

"Yeah, leave me alone." I fought back tears. I was ten years old again being taunted by Peter. "I just buried my mother."

"Well, she must have been some mother to have a son like you."

I wondered where such hatred and evil came from. I wondered what terrible mother produced *him*. Back in my apartment, I tried to put the asshole out of my mind, but I was sure he could hear every move I made. I was filled with rage and hatred about what he'd said about my mother. I paced the floors. I decided to go to an AA meeting to vent my anger and frustrations. The next one was close by and started in a half-hour. I poured my heart out about my neighbor and how he was making my life miserable and explained what I had been through with my mother. At the meeting was a friend, Mike, who was also a friend of Tom Duane. Tom was a New York City Council member who later became the only openly gay HIV-positive state senator in the New York State

Legislature. When Mike heard the story, he went home after the meeting and called Tom and told him what was going on. Later that day, I got a call. "Mark, this is Tom Duane. Mike told me what was happening and I'm worried about you. What you've described at the meeting sounds like a hate crime. I'm going to have my office look into it." He also gave me a number of the Anti-Gay Violence Project.

I thanked him and wrote down the number, but I was still pretty skeptical. After all, I still had to live next door to this asshole. My friend Kevin was a member of the NYPD. Kevin told me to file a complaint about each incident separately, dating back to the first incident. The police at the precinct were very nice to me, a marked change since I tried to file a complaint against Steven Pines. I filed two separate complaints and hoped for the best. The next day was Election Day. The Associated Blind Building, where everyone votes, was across the street, so I walked over to cast my vote. There in the line waiting to vote was my redneck neighbor. He glared at me. I thought he was going to burst into a rage at any moment. He wouldn't stop staring.

Everyone I knew in the neighborhood where I lived for fifteen years came up and said 'hi' to me. My downstairs neighbor, Rita, hugged me and said how sorry she was about my mom. The neighbor down the hall and her young son came up and greeted me. The doorman, Sam, shook my hand and expressed his condolences and so did many others. This display of affection from the neighbors seemed to enrage Unger even more.

I waited for him to vote and leave before walking home. I was already in my apartment when I heard his door slam as he returned home. He went crazy banging on the walls so hard I thought he'd break every glass object on my shelves. I took the Art Deco glass down and just sat there. I could hear him throwing things against the walls, kicking the furniture and then banging on the walls again. His rampage ended in an eerie silence.

I was afraid to leave my apartment. I was no match for this guy. If he wanted to, he could hurt me. I hid silently in my apartment. The next day, my neighbor received two letters in the mail, one from the City Council's Office and one from the AGVP. They were both carbon copied to my co-op board, the NYPD and me.

> Dear Tom Unger:
>
> Our office is aware that two police reports have been filed against you, alleging that you have threatened another individual, using anti-gay slurs. We consider this a bias crime and this office will do everything in its power to see that these complaints are prosecuted to the fullest extent under the laws of New York Cit and the State of New York.
>
> Tom Duane, City Councilman
>
> Matt Forman, Anti-Gay Violence Project

I was working when one of the receptionists told me I had a phone call.

"Is this Mark Okun?" He said in an irate tone.

"Yes, it is. Who's calling?"

"This is Mr. Unger. Apparently, you've taken it upon yourself to file some complaints against my son, Tom Unger. My son told me all about what's been going on over there with you complaining to the co-op board and harassing him. This is an outrage that you are using taxpayers' money to file unwarranted complaints against my son—hiding behind these bias crime laws! I'm going to sue you."

I let him scream on.

"What about my son's civil rights? He has a right to live in peace without your noise and harassment. I don't think you know who you're dealing with."

I interjected, "Mr. Unger, knock yourself out. You and your son can go ahead and sue me. I'd like nothing better than to watch you go broke paying for your lawyers."

The co-op board called a meeting to resolve the problem between us. It was to be held the following week at 4:30 pm. The President of the board and the two board members, myself, Unger, his girlfriend and his father were present. The President and I already knew each other from me complaining about Mr. Unger's behavior. He seemed determined to resolve this once and for all. The president of the board stayed in Unger's apartment with Unger, his girlfriend and father and sent Rita and me with the other two board members into my apartment. They told me to turn on my stereo. They had me turn it louder and louder until it was on much louder than I normally would have played it. All that the president could hear from Tom's apartment was the bass and that was only audible when the music was turned far beyond normal levels. After the demonstration, the president turned to Unger and said, "Mr. Unger, Mr. Okun has the right to make reasonable noise between the hours of 8:00 am and 11:00 pm; it's New York City law. This feud has gone on long enough. It's time for you to get on with your life."

Unger countered, "I swear, it's louder when he plays it."

"We've made our determination. I suggest you apologize to Mr. Okun and both of you put this behind you."

He looked at me with a punk smirk on his face and said, "Okay, look, I'm sorry, okay…"

"Yeah, sure," I said, but I still couldn't forgive him for what he said about my mother.

We shook hands. They say that what doesn't kill you, will only make you stronger. How fucking strong do you have to be?

MAKEOVERS YOU'LL NEVER FORGET

I was back on my boat "The Sylvia" in Fire Island Pines. I had just gotten over my most recent failed relationship. I went decided to go to an AA meeting in The Pines, to catch up with friends and share about how I was feeling. I came in late and the meeting had already started. A tall, older guy with lots of muscles was starting to speak. His face lit up when I entered the room. "Hi, I'm John and I'm an alcoholic. I'm forty-nine years old and I'm finally able to go out to a club dancing. Since I've been sober, I would only go to the gym or the grocery store or be home by myself."

After the meeting, he lingered for a few minutes. He paused to look in my direction and then abruptly turned and walked towards town. I followed him. It looked like he went into the grocery store, so I went inside. Pretending to shop for groceries, I kept throwing things in my cart, searching the aisles for him. He wasn't anywhere in the store. Quickly I replaced all the groceries back on the shelves. Outside, there he was, standing on the boardwalk in front of the Boatel. I ran up and introduced myself. With a beautiful, wide smile, he told me his name was John. After our introduction, he grew quiet and stared at me uncomfortably, waiting for me to say something else.

"Do you see that boat across the harbor? If you look over there across the harbor, you can see it from here. That's where I live on the weekends. I've been coming here for sixteen years. I don't think I've ever seen you here before."

"Maybe you have, but you've just never noticed me before."

I felt like I had to keep the conversation going because his answers were short and concise and he didn't volunteer much information on his own. He'd flash me that movie star smile, though, and it encouraged me to find out more about him. Unfortunately, I was leaving later that day to attend a wedding in the city. The bride, Cindy produced a talk show. "John, I wish we had more time. Come by next weekend and I'll take you for a boat ride."

"Okay."

At that moment it occurred to me that Luis's hot Argentinean bodybuilder boyfriend, Christian, who had been crowned "Mr. Argentina" was coming to stay with me on the boat next weekend. "Listen, John, if you see a good looking Latin guy on the boat, he's a friend—not my boyfriend. So don't be afraid. Come over."

Saturday morning I was drinking coffee on the deck and trying to carry on a conversation with Christian, who barely spoke English. I heard someone clear his throat and I looked up to see John flashing me that movie star smile. I welcomed him aboard and we took a ride around the Great South Bay. Between the noise of the boat and John's shy demeanor, the conversation was difficult to keep going. When we were back in the slip, we made a date to go dancing that evening. John was quite affectionate and the evening went really well.

Because of Christian staying on the boat and the lack of privacy, we had sex up on the deck, but John couldn't stay over and I didn't want to go to his house. John called the next day to say what a nice time he'd had. I felt comfortable with him and soon we were dating regularly. John's month lease was up on his Fire Island house and he was without a place to stay for two weeks, until the lease on his new house started. I invited him to stay with me for the weekend on my boat. He flew out on a seaplane, arriving with a small duffle bag full of clothes.

There were some details to work out. Being 6'1" myself, I barely fit on my own boat. The bathroom was so small I had to kick the door open to get my pants back up. In the cabin there was only a six-foot ceiling in the galley, which got lower and lower toward the bow. John was 6'4" and solid muscle. He was a really good sport about it.

He was very polite, but I got the feeling that there was something strange about him. Somehow, he didn't seem quite fully connected. We began to spend a lot of time together in the city, as well as on Fire Island. One night during the week, I was at his apartment when he was trying to straighten out the CDs on his shelves. He had about five thousand CDs, all arranged in alphabetical order, in specially designed cabinets. When I asked him what was wrong, he snapped at me and kept on with what he was doing. He was acting really weird. Up to now, he'd been so nice. I figured it was too good to be true. I wondered if I should just get out now, while I had the chance, but I decided to wait and see. The next weekend on Fire Island, I had some women friends from Memphis for a visit. They were salon people I knew from flying there once a month to cut hair. I'd invited them to come and stay with me on the boat. John had rented a beautiful house on the ocean with a beautiful pool, high ceilings with ceiling fans, a gorgeous blue tile floor and four spacious bedrooms. He wanted me to come and stay there with him, but I didn't like to leave my friends in the harbor. John came down to the harbor with me to greet the women from Memphis. He looked at all their luggage and shook his head in disbelief. "There's no way you women are going to fit on Mark's little boat. You're all going to have to come and stay with me at my house. There'll be plenty of room there for you and your luggage. I won't take 'no' for an answer."

He was the most gracious and generous host for the rest of the weekend. Seeing the incredible acts of kindness John was capable of I began to fall in love with him. John was part owner in a gym called 'David Barton's' in the city and lived off his investments. I thought he must be wealthy to be able to rent such a big and beautiful rental home right on the ocean in The Pines. I saw the real estate agent carrying his bags and bowing and scraping whenever John flew into town on the seaplane. An acquaintance, who knew him, said his family's money came from oil.

I spent more time with John and began to worry about the strange demons that troubled him. He seemed moody and he cleaned and straightened everything to excess. John's cleanliness went far beyond the norm. I asked him, "John, what's wrong with you? Why do you torture yourself like this? Sit down and just leave everything alone. You're driving yourself crazy."

"I have OCD. Because of it, I've had a hard time functioning all my life. I could barely work but since my family has money, I didn't have to. It's hereditary. My grandmother had it. "In an attempt to self-medicate, I began drinking. At first it relaxed me, but with my family's predisposition for alcoholism, my drinking soon escalated. I'd find myself places and not know how I got there. After years of drinking and one bout in a mental hospital, I found AA. I've been sober now for thirteen years."

I began to learn more about OCD. Around the same time, OCD became a popular topic on TV news shows. Howard Stern admitted that he had it. The film *As Good as It Gets* stars Jack Nicholson as a man with OCD. I began to understand that people with OCD see the world as an out-of-control place. By performing their compulsive rituals, such as washing their hands over and over or rearranging canned goods in a cabinet, they are making order out of chaos. Psychiatrists also discovered that some antidepressants (Zoloft) work well on OCD. For a person with OCD, letting go is like losing control to them. I encouraged John to try some of the new medications. Once he found one that worked and with cognitive therapy, he began to grow as a person. He made friends much more easily and didn't shy away from social situations that used to overwhelm him. He could now comfortably handle the little things that used to drive him crazy. I like to think I played a small part in his recovery.

I began to realize how much I loved John. I couldn't imagine life without him. He was becoming my best friend, as well as my lover.

John has stuck with me in good times and in bad (and didn't leave me when I got a little fat.) When someone helps you grow as a person and sees you at your worst and still loves you, that is what love is about. It's easy to love someone if you only see him or her at their best. I hope John will stay with me and hold my hand, as we grew old, for however long that would be.

Loving and living with John required me to make certain adjustments. What he lacks in some areas, he makes up for in others. If I had met John when I was younger and caught up in the frenzy of lust, drugs and rock and roll, I would never have noticed him. I would never have been able to stick it out and get beyond his anxiety and compulsive behavior, to his warm and giving nature. Sometimes, John's medications don't work as well as they should and he makes me really crazy. Other times he's so sweet, I feel I must be the luckiest guy in the world.

I told John, "I wish you didn't have OCD."

He answered, "I wish you didn't have HIV." We may not exactly be the "Gay Poster Couple," but one day at a time, the days turn into years.

A SHORT JEW
IN THE BODY OF A TALL WASP

As I walked into my apartment, the phone was ringing. My friend Mindy seemed drunk. As usual. I could barely understand what she was saying. It sounded like, "I've got your sister on the other line," which freaked me out. I never had a sister.

"Mark, this is your sister Charlene. I've been looking for you for a long time," said an unfamiliar voice. Until that moment, I had been pretty sure of my identity. I always thought my birth mother would be Jewish even though I always knew from the way I looked I'd only be part Jewish. It was such a shock to find out I wasn't Jewish at all.

When I got on the phone I was a Jew; when I got off I was a Goy!

With Mindy, I had half-heartedly been searching for my birth family for several months. From the outset Mindy was more concerned with finding my birth mother than I was. I'd met Mindy about ten years ago. Both our parents had died and we had no other siblings. Mindy's mother had died of cancer, leaving Mindy with a large sum of money, but no other living relatives. She moved to Boca Raton, Florida soon after. It wasn't until I bought an apartment in Miami that we really got to know each other. After my mother died I used my inheritance to buy an apartment in Miami for $35,000 with a water view, even though it was over a garage. I thought if I got sick, I could go there and live cheaply. Business was bad for a while and I thought maybe I'd move sooner. A client of mine pointed out that if I left New York, I could never have back what I had now, if I changed my mind. So I decided to go one week a month and see if it is what I want to do. Business in New York got better. I liked being in Miami once a month. I always want to be a New Yorker. It gives you an edge over everyone else. I had my adoption papers and shared this information with Mindy. We knew the adoption lawyer's name and my birth name—Mark Brecht. We also knew that my birth family was from upstate New York. I believe Mindy was chasing her own need for family by helping me find mine. From the moment I told her about finding my adoption papers, she seemed to be on a crusade. Mindy spent a lot of time at home watching talk shows on TV because she had nothing better to do. One day I called her in Boca and she sounded upset. I asked her what was wrong. "I'm watching Sally Jesse Raphael," she sniffled, "and on the show, guests are being reunited on TV with their birth parents. Mark, wouldn't you like to find out who your birth parents are? Aren't you curious about whom they are, if they are still alive?"

"Mindy, I think you're getting a little obsessed with the whole idea, aren't you? I don't really have the time to do it. And besides, how much is all this going to cost?" I really wondered how much it was going to cost me emotionally. I guess every child who is adopted thinks, "What does my birth mother look like? Why did she give me up? Does she think about me? What would my life have been like if I had my real parents?" Never having looked like anyone in my family I longed to look at someone and see myself in them. I had my own reasons for never having tried to find my birth family before. I loved my adoptive parents, Abe and Sylvia. I felt that if I tried to find my birth family, it would have killed them. While they were alive I never would have done it out of respect for them.

But Mindy was persistent, so she called the agency from the talk show. She explained, "They're backed up for two years and they have a waiting list. There are a lot of people trying to find their birth parents now, it seems."

"I'm curious but not enough to put a lot of time into it. I feel totally complete just the way I am."

"Mark, you'll always wonder if you never find out. I know you never wanted to disrespect your parents, but now they're dead. You can't hurt them anymore. They would want you to have a new family."

"What if they don't want to know me? I think you just don't have anything better to do with yourself."

My own curiosity got the better of me. I finally called the number that Mindy gave me. I reached a man who explained that there was another way to go. There was a kit available that I could buy for two hundred fifty dollars. It gave you forms to find your birth family in every state. If after one and a half years I still had not found my birth family, I could retain the agency for an additional fifteen hundred dollars and would receive a two hundred fifty dollar credit for the cost of the kit. I gave my credit card number to order it. Mindy took over from there. Despite my excuses, she started making phone calls on her own. In a million years, I never thought she would really find them.

I had spent many years searching for something that would make me feel complete. I had taken a giant step toward that when I got on the phone for the first time with my half-sister Charlene. I couldn't believe my ears. She had asked me, "Were you born on May 1, 1954 at Crouse Irving Hospital in Syracuse, New York?"

I was.

Charlene was sixty-two. My mother was still alive and eighty-two. I had three brothers, nieces, a nephew—it was all too much for me. She said she'd been looking for me, but considering how long it took her to find me I gathered it wasn't a very thorough search. That was all right though. After all, I hadn't done anything. I was grateful just to hear her voice. I'd known other adopted kids who'd spent years searching for their birth families, only to be devastated by the discovery that the families wanted nothing to do with them. At least their people wanted to know who I was, and most important of all, wanted me to know them. I was grateful to Mindy for finding them. "Mark, I don't think we should tell your birth mother Alice about you quite yet, She's very old and her heart is not very strong. I am afraid the shock of it all would kill her."

"Well, then, just tell me about her."

Charlene proceeded, "Alice was a good mother. I was very close to her. She was married to a man who was of German descent. He served in the military and then worked as a carpenter. He was a hard drinking kind of guy and he died young. After he died, Alice found out about his fooling around. She was hurt and felt very angry and betrayed.

"There was military base near our home called Fort Drum. Alice began hanging around the base going on dates with some of the soldiers. One of them was a captain from the base, very handsome, tall, blonde, blue-eyed and heavy. I only met him once, but I remember him because of his Scandinavian looks. Shortly after this, my aunt and my grandparents sent Alice to live with another aunt in Syracuse while the children and I stayed in Watertown with our grandmother. They said she had to go there to work for a few months.

"While Alice was living in Syracuse, my fiancé and I became engaged. I was a twenty-one year old, soon-to-be bride and was dying to tell the good news to my mother. So I got a bus to Syracuse. When I got to my aunt's house, my mother answered the door! I almost fainted. I didn't even know she was pregnant.

"She told me that the family could not allow the shame of a child born out of wedlock. Being Christian, she had no choice but to have the child and give it up for adoption. She said there was a lawyer in Syracuse who knew of a Jewish couple who could not have children. Alice approved of this arrangement because she thought that Jews were wealthy and the child could have what she could not give. She didn't seem upset at all. But I was terribly upset."

I could barely absorb all this information, but I was hungry for more. Now I knew where I got my blonde hair, my solid stature and my blue eyes. Now I realized that my genes had been at war with my upbringing.

Whenever Barbara Eden was in New York, I would do her hair for various TV appearances. One day I accompanied her to the studio for the *Geraldo Show*, which was taping "Hit TV Shows of the 60s." As we walked inside the studio, we were introduced to Cindy, the producer, whom I recognized as a neighbor from the same co-op I lived in. Thinking this was my big break I invited Cindy to come to the salon where

I worked for a free haircut hoping that she would love her hair and out of gratitude give me a makeover show. I was convinced that if you got a makeover on a talk show, people would see how good you were and the trip to hairdresser stardom would be only a blink away.

I started doing her hair regularly, but the show never materialized. Instead she got me some odd jobs on the Geraldo Show, like putting disguise wigs on guests who didn't want their neighbors to know what sleaze bags they were. I would go to all these wig stores and borrow wigs in return for getting them credit on the show. Then I'd run over to the studio, plop the wig on the guest and bill the show for two hundred, fifty dollars, which wasn't bad for less than an hour's work. Other times I was hired to comb out celebrities such as Nicole Miller, Claudia Cohen, Marla Maples, Patty Duke and Ivana Trump, whom I didn't have to do anything to because she came camera ready. So, I got paid for doing nothing. Cindy had me cut Geraldo's hair and I thought he was a real nice guy. The whole thing was an acid trip without any drugs.

After several years, Cindy left Geraldo for a better job as executive producer for the Gordon Elliot Show. But I still longed for a makeover show and the chance at fame. In her new position, Cindy promised me a makeover show if I thought of an original idea. She was desperate for ideas because she was producing five shows a week,.

"How about prenatal makeover," I ventured.

"Done before," she replied.

"Makeovers for the handicapped?"

"People don't want to watch handicapped people get made over."

"Twins?"

"Done before."

"You know how I told you I was adopted and just talked to my birth family on the phone for the first time, but haven't met them yet. How about if I meet them for the first time on the show and after that I do everyone's hair?"

"You got the show."

Cindy wasted no time in making it a reality. The day before the show, I kept myself busy calling all my friends asking them to be in the audience of the Gordon Elliot Show. With the preparations for the next day, I wasn't focusing on the big picture of what was about to happen. That night the reality hit me. As I undressed and stepped into the shower, tears just poured out. I missed my parents, the parents who raised me—the people I knew were my real parents. I didn't want to meet these people who never really wanted me anyway. I wanted Abe and Sylvia. They were the ones who had raised me, fed me, cared for me when I was sick; accepted me even when they saw that I was different. But now they were gone. I was alone now with only what they had taught me. It would prove to be my best inheritance.

I dried myself off and looked in the bathroom mirror. My blue eyes were swollen and red. My blonde hair stood up in wet tufts like the great lawn after a polo match. What a TV debut this will be, I thought. In my eagerness to further my career, I had overlooked the emotional magnitude. What could these new people do for me now, but further confuse me about who I really am? How did I know this new family would accept me, when they found out who I was, when they found out I was gay? I was happy with the parents I had. I didn't want new parents.

I thought I was nervous about being on TV, but I realized that it was scary for me to meet my birth family. I didn't know very much about them except that they came from a small, depressed town called Watertown in upstate New York. I pictured a whole family of trailer trash. I knew one thing for sure—if I looked out there and they didn't have teeth, I wasn't coming out!

The next morning, the sky was gray but it wasn't raining. It was a typical drab March day in New York. I managed to put myself together so that when I looked in the mirror, I was acceptable. I was told to wear something bright because that would look better on television.

My best friend Phyllis knocked at the door. She was dressed in black, New York City chic, stiletto heels and a trench coat. She worked for Chanel now, and her makeup was dramatic that day—dark, smoky eyes, contrasting with her platinum blonde Debbie Harry hair and pouty red lips. We took a cab to the theater together. Cindy accompanied us to the back room. She insisted that my friend Mindy appear on the show with me, since Mindy was the one who actually located my family and Cindy loved the human-interest part of the story. They stuck us in a makeshift dressing room underneath a staircase.

I was worried about how Mindy would do on stage. She didn't want to be on TV. When I told her about the makeover and my idea of meeting my family on a talk show, she had gotten really upset. She came up with every excuse possible not to do it, but I knew why she really didn't want to be on TV If my hands shook like hers when I needed a drink, I'd be nervous about going on TV too. She managed to put herself together pretty well. At least she didn't have on one of those Laura Ashley baby doll dresses she usually wore with those bobby socks. Phyllis took out her bag of Chanel make-up and went to work on Mindy. By the time she was finished, Mindy reminded me a little of Joan Crawford, in "All About Eve." We were all a little nervous for our own reasons, but, for better or worse, another of our adventures was about to begin.

As I was about to meet my birth family, I wondered if they would have even chosen to appear on the show if they had known about my wild early years. But what I wondered even more was whether I would have turned out to be the same rebellious, wild guy if we had been raised together and shared the same humble background. An assistant producer poked his head in the dressing room and informed us that it was time to go on. Mindy and I took our seats on the stage. Gordon Elliot, a big, swaggering Aussie chap broke the ice by making a joke about us starting a new sitcom, "Mark and Mindy."

Gordon leaned in close and started asking some background questions. He turned to Mindy and asked how we began the quest to find my birth parents. She told how a reunion show on TV sucked her in and how we sent away for the kit from International Locators. Then it was my turn in the hot seat. He asked why I didn't do this myself. I told him how complex the kit looked. I described my adopted parents as looking like Dr. Ruth and Mario Cuomo. The audience laughed. The crowd seemed interested in what I had to say, probably because about sixty of them were my friends.

It was time for my birth family to make their appearance. They filed onto the stage—first my half-sister Charlene (who looked old enough to be my mother), followed by my half-brothers Howard, Jerry and John. We all embraced, but I was thinking, "These people are hicks. I'll never see them again after the show." Charlene, who was a little on the assertive side, was the self-appointed spokesperson for the family, interrupting whenever anyone tried to talk so she could clarify and explain how it really was. She interrupted Gordon Elliot at one point! When they took a break to show pictures of me as a youngster and Abe and Sylvia when they were young, my eyes welled with tears.

The woman who gave me life slowly made her entrance. I was struck by the fact that she was wearing a necklace with one of the biggest crosses I had ever seen. Even nuns don't wear crosses that big! I heard the collective gasps of my Jewish friends in the audience. I knew Alice was aware I was Jewish.

I walked up to her and gave her a big hug and a kiss, realizing how frail she was. She gripped my arm tightly for support and I helped her to her seat. Gordon kneeled down next to her and kidded her about her five marriages and her out-of-wedlock child, calling me her "love puppy." He asked her why she gave me up for adoption. She just said, "It was too much." She seemed embarrassed and at a loss for words.

After an uncomfortable silence, Charlene chimed in and explained, "Her mother and sister forced her to give up Mark because back then it was shameful to have a child outside of wedlock. My mom gave him up because she wasn't able to give him the life he deserved."

I kept glancing at Alice to see if we looked alike. It seemed that we resembled each other more closely than she did her other children. Now I know what I'll look like when I'm eighty-two.

Gordon informed my birth family that I had a surprise for them. I told them that I wanted to give all the women—my half-sister, my mother, and my half-brothers' wives—a makeover they'd never forget, a day of beauty at my salon, so that they could see firsthand what I did for a living. They were thrilled at the prospect and we went by stretch limo to the Donsuki Salon to meet the expert team of colorists, make-up artists and fashion consultants. I thought of the current play that was on Off Broadway, *I Love You Just as You Are, Now Change*.

En route to the salon with my birth family, I considered what a different man I had become. As I looked at my birth mother, my sister and brothers, I made mental notes for the upcoming makeovers. They really did need a good makeover. I have a habit of making over just about everyone I meet. Even the most glamorous could use a little help. My birth family, however, needed a lot of help. I was to do my mother's, my birth sisters' and my sisters-in-law's hair and makeup. Fashion consultants provided them with new clothes. The pace was fast with so many of them to do at once. I stared in awe as I finally saw the strong, physical family resemblance. With their hair wet and everyone more relaxed, I could see that not only did I resemble them physically, but also my facial expressions and speech patterns were similar. For some reason, this annoyed me rather than endearing them to me. As I was doing my birth mother's hair, I looked at her face. She had my eyes, my mouth and lips, my nose and cheekbones. This was my face, I thought, as I looked at the familiar features. If it weren't for this woman, I wouldn't exist. This was the face of my mother. But not the mother who stayed up all night with me when I had a fever, who made sure I ate my broccoli, who helped me with my homework and who worried about me when I came home late. Alice wasn't the mother who put me before herself, like Sylvia had...but then again, I guess she did.

Everyone made over, we pranced back onto the stage, I took another really good look at these people who were my new family. I reconsidered my earlier attitude of not wanting anything to do with them after the show was over. I already felt a sort of familiarity, a bond beginning to connect me to them. I wanted to know more about them before dismissing them as not worth knowing. Maybe they could provide some of the answers to the questions I had about myself. Or maybe they could just enrich my life by providing me with a family now that my parents were no longer with me.

I still think of myself as a Jew. Half of my friends are Jewish and I relate to them in a special way because of our shared Jewish heritage. Now with Abe and Sylvia gone, and realizing I had no Jewish blood at all, I wondered if I would still continue to think of myself as a Jew. One of my Southern clients had told me, "Don't you know no one wants to be Jewish?"

Upon learning of my reunion with my Christian birth mother, my mother-in-law (John's mother) reacted "Oh, good, now you can come to church with us for Easter."

When I drop something, I still say 'Oy'. I still feel like a Jew. I wanted to know my birth family, but that didn't change who I was or my upbringing. I am a short Jew in the body of a tall WASP.

When my birth mother sat beside me on the set of the Gordon Elliot Show and I took her hand in mine, I was overcome with emotion. Meeting the person who brought me into the world was overwhelming. I never felt any anger or resentment towards her, ever. But I just thought these people were hicks. I have nothing in common with them. Sophia's comment to me after the show was "Darling, now we have something else in common. Both our mothers have been married five times." I replied, "Yea, but your mother keeps marrying aristocrats and my mother just married mailmen."

I threw a party at my apartment after the show so all my friends could meet my new family. The next day, John took the whole family to Rockefeller Center to have lunch while watching the ice skaters. After lunch, Alice, my birth mother, started having difficulties breathing. She was throwing up and couldn't breathe. Charlene, my 'new' sister, became very concerned. We decided we better get her to a hospital. I couldn't believe it. Now, just twenty-four hours after meeting my birth mother, I was rushing her to intensive care. "Oh, please," I thought, "I've done this already."

I made some phone calls to a friend of a friend who was a doctor on call at the hospital. My new family was very impressed at how capable and in control I was, but after all my experiences, it just came naturally. The Gordon Elliot Show had only paid for two nights in the hotel for the family, so the rest of the family went back to Watertown, while my half-sister, Charlene, her son Dan, and my younger half-brother, John, stayed in my apartment. Alice had forgotten to take her medications and had developed arterial fibrillation. The doctors wanted to keep her in the hospital and watch her for a week. She seemed to be doing better as the days progressed and they moved her out of intensive care. Sharing this stressful situation with my new siblings Char, Dan and John seemed to bond us in a special way. I felt guilty for judging them and thinking of them as hicks. Char talked extensively about the family, filling in the gaps and satisfying my need to know all about them. Since they had met me with John and never knew me without him, they seemed to think of us as a long-term couple, even though John and I had only been together for a year at that point. I liked the way they accepted us right away. I couldn't believe I was lucky enough to have two families that accepted me being gay. I knew many people whose families never accepted them and I saw how this lack of acceptance manifested itself in self-hatred.

The following April, John and I went up to Watertown to see my birth family. They threw me a huge party with a giant banner on the side of my nephew's house that read, "Happy Birthday, Uncle Mark." It was very moving. I loved having nieces and nephews, all sixteen of them. My birth family was less fortunate than I and it was somewhat of a culture shock for me to see the way they lived. The thing that struck me the most, however, was that this could've been my life. They thought I was some kind of movie star. This wasn't because I grew up very affluent—I didn't. My parents were solidly middle class.

If you think of the world as a place where there is not enough, then it will become a self-fulfilling prophecy. But if you think of the world as a place of abundance, you'll always receive what you need. My Grandma Fanny taught me as a little boy to look at the world as a place of opportunity, of goals waiting to be obtained. My extended Jewish family achieved all kinds of things in their lives. No one in my birth family had succeeded past a certain point. So, they didn't believe it was possible.

All the members of my new family are Protestant, except for Char, who had converted to Catholicism. One of her sons converted also. His name was David and he became a priest. I invited David to come to New York for dinner while he was finishing at seminary school in Philadelphia. David came up on the train just for the day. Phyllis and I took him to St. Patrick's Cathedral. We went back to my apartment before leaving for dinner. Phyllis tried to ask questions about the circumstance of my birth. I wondered what it was like to be a priest—to devote your whole life to God and never have sex!

"My mom always felt neglected by my grandmother. Alice was a kind woman, and although she wasn't abusive, my mother thought of her as neglectful. Her interests and energy were totally focused on her social life. She wasn't as involved as she could have been raising her daughter. My mom, being oldest, always had to look out for her brothers and herself as Grandma's husbands and boyfriends came and went.

"Alice was married five times. After her second husband, Mr. Brecht, died, Alice found out he had been unfaithful to her. Reacting to her feelings of betrayal, she began to date a few guys from the army base at Fort Drum. My mother walked in on Alice with a man (your father) and another woman. My mom never really got over it."

This was almost too much to take. Here I was, a Jew, with a priest for a nephew, who was telling me I had been conceived during a three way! It took me a week to recover. His story shocked even jaded Phyllis. I am always surprised by the self-righteousness and intolerance of many very religious people. Who am I to judge anyone? I've certainly done worse things. The God I believe in doesn't want us to judge others because everyone's set of circumstances is different. Religion should be 'do good, feel good; do bad, feel badly.' All the rest is bullshit. No one knows who God is or what he does or doesn't like.

I'm sure Alice's heart had been broken many times and she must have been very brave to keep trying again. I think she finally found it with her last husband, Carl. Is she less noble than another woman who spends forty years with a man she hates? Sylvia was very lucky to have found Abe the first time around. Not everyone can be that lucky.

I once asked Alice if she could remember something about my father, she said, "I just can't remember. Isn't that terrible?"

"Don't worry," I replied. "I can't remember half the people I slept with either."

HAVE SCISSORS, WILL TRAVEL

I was afraid that all the stress I'd been through had taken its toll on my immune system. When I had my blood work done, however, my T-cell levels remained the same. I still went regularly to AA meetings for HIV positive people, which helped to keep me grounded. The small meeting on Houston Street, which I helped found, was like group therapy, and they gave me the strength I needed to live in a world where everyone was still sick and dying. My friend, Carl, from Fire Island, became so sick that his new lover could no longer care for him. Carl's mother and brother made arrangements for him to come home to North Carolina for his final months. Bedridden, he told me on the phone, "I'm not afraid to die, Mark, but the pain is almost unbearable. The doctors have promised me they're going to give me a morphine drip and that I can control myself. Hopefully, this will stop the pain."

"Carl, I just can't understand how you got so sick, so fast. Your blood tests were always so much better than mine and you were so much healthier than I was when we both were first tested."

I never imagined Carl would get so sick and die before me. His mother wrote me a ten-page letter after his death, documenting his last days of life in excruciating detail, ending with the words, "I hope when you get sick it won't be as bad."

Out of the eighteen people who lived in our Fire Island house, only three were still alive. Two weren't positive, and then there was me. My clientele had dwindled after my mother's death. Many of my clients left to follow the colorist, Barry, to the new salon, this left big holes in my daily schedule. Clients always wanted the busiest, hottest hairdresser. When they saw that I wasn't as busy, they assumed I was no longer hot and went chasing whoever they perceived to be the new trendsetter. They say when things are bad, that's when you find out who your friends are. Clients who I thought would be loyal, dropped me and other people who I didn't really think about much stood by me. I was hard pressed to find new ways to expand my clientele and make more money.

One of my most loyal clients and friends, Mike Cannon, helped me out of my nosedive by introducing me to some important new women. Mike was Editor-at-Large for *Town & Country Magazine* and the job suited him well. He often listened to my tales of woe, chain smoking and drinking one Diet Pepsi after another. To say he was high-strung would be an understatement. Mike was born and raised in Memphis and was well acquainted with the wealthy, opulent way of life that his magazine represented. He had a large circle of friends from his hometown, Memphis that included many very wealthy old families. Mike got me styling jobs working with him for the magazine. I did Princess Yasmin Aga Khan's hair for the Alzheimer's Gala in 1992. We made her look exactly the way her mother, Rita Hayworth, looked fifty years earlier for the cover of *Town & Country* in 1942.

I also did Mary Fisher's hair when Town & Country made her Woman of the Year. Mary Fisher was a wealthy white

Republican, who contracted HIV from her husband. I knew her parents from Palm Beach, Marjorie and Max Fisher. She lectured throughout the country on HIV and AIDS. She even addressed the Republican National Convention. She could have remained anonymous and sheltered from the pain of admitting to the public that she had been exposed to this disease. She was always portrayed as an "innocent victim." I always resented this. We are all innocent victims of this disease. Even though we now know that the unprotected sex promoted the spread of the disease, we didn't know it before AIDS. Being gay, black or poor shouldn't make a person any more "guilty" or deserving of the fate than someone like Mary Fisher, a heterosexual, wealthy, white woman.

Just the same, I was thrilled to meet her and I thought it was wonderful that Town & Country bestowed this honor upon her. In that circle, it took a lot of courage to openly admit her HIV status.

I enjoyed working with Mike and with Town & Country. They even did write-ups about me from time to time. They called me "The Traveling Hairdresser." But, aside from the photo shoots I did, my steady clientele was not enough to sustain me at my income level. Mike started referring his wealthy southern lady friends to me whenever they came to the city. They were such characters. There were two clients in particular who were influential in my career. One was Pat Cook, a beautiful blonde ex-model from Memphis, who now resided in Palm Beach. The other was Mrs. Jean Price, who still lives in Memphis and who became a good friend to me. Pat Cook met Edward Cook whose family made its fortune on the Cotton Exchange, when she was his secretary. He left his wife for her. She loved the first time I cut her hair in a short hip style. It took years off the matronly, conservative style she had worn. All her friends in Palm Beach started asking who did her hair.

Since I already owned a condo in Miami, and was visiting Florida on a monthly basis anyway, I drove the one and a half hours to Palm Beach to cut Mrs. Cook's and her friends' hair at her home. While they were getting their hair cut, she had a jewelry show from New York going on in the dining room, which was the size of a bowling alley. It was just like a Tupperware party, but with diamonds. When I first arrived at the Cook's house, I tried to conceal my astonishment. I had never before been in a house as big and as expensively decorated. I felt like I didn't belong there and that I would soon be found out. It was a twenty-five room, Spanish-style mansion, with rooms the size of gymnasiums. Mrs. Cook kept a staff of two butlers, two maids, a major domo, a handyman and a personal secretary. She seemed to love all the activity at her home and the role of hostess. I was introduced all around and after I was done with each woman's hair, they seemed thrilled at their hot new looks.

One of the women I met was Mrs. Carol Carpenter. She was related to the DuPont family and once flown me down to Palm Beach just to do her hair. When I arrived late one evening, Mrs. Carpenter told me I should go swimming in her pool. I felt uncomfortable because I really didn't know them that well yet.

"Well, no really, I didn't bring a suit."

"We won't peek."

I was really thinking if they knew I was HIV positive, I'm sure they'd drain the pool!

I felt like I needed a Rolls Royce and a pacemaker to fit in.

Mrs. Carpenter had me come to Wilmington, Delaware once to do her hair. She couldn't come to New York because she had to stay with her husband who was recuperating from knee surgery. I looked at the request as an adventure, each thing leading to another, and the money was good. I was told to take the train to Wilmington Station. Their handyman picked me up in a green Jaguar and whooshed me to their estate. We passed Winterthur, the DuPont ancestral home that is now a museum and arrived at a secluded wooded area where her home was situated. It was a beautiful Georgian mansion with a grand ballroom and high cathedral ceilings. "Thank you so much for coming, Mark. You're my savior; I feel so much better now that you're here. Do you think you can choose which one of these dresses suits me best and then try to do something with my hair? You're such a genius." I cut and styled her hair so it looked fabulous. Her hair was naturally thin on top but I found a way to let it bush out while trimming the sides. I picked out a dress that would best frame her neck and face. The whole thing took less than an hour and she was ready to send me on my way back home.

"You did a fabulous job. How much do I owe you?" she asked.

I knew what I usually charged for a haircut in the salon or for a house call. I wanted five hundred dollars, I thought, but I would take three-fifty because I thought she was a good connection. "I really don't know what to charge," I said.

"I know what I'll do. Have a safe trip back to New York." She handed me an envelope. I put it into my pocked without opening it, thanked her and left. I didn't open it until I sat down to wait for my train at the station. I pulled it out of my pocket, opened the envelope and started counting the bills.

I nearly fainted. There was fifteen hundred dollars in one hundred dollar bills.

I was soon doing almost everyone's hair in Palm Beach—Kathy Ford, Lidia Mann, Virginia Mulholland, Liz Gillette, Kit Panel, Mrs. Harrison, Priscilla Pochna, Mrs. Ray Floyd, Andy Phipps and one of my favorites, Mrs. Don Shula of Miami Beach. Once while doing Mrs. Carpenter's hair, I overheard her talking on the phone to Elizabeth Dole. I could tell by the conversation she was asking her to endorse Bob in his candidacy for President. Mrs. Carpenter asked Mrs. Dole, "Is Newt giving Bob a hard time?" Being a liberal Democrat all my life, steam came out of my ears, but then I began to feel like Robin Hood. I was taking from the right to give to the left (me).

If I had too many clients in Palm Beach to do in one day, I'd stay overnight at Mindy's and finish my customers the next day. This is when we really got to know each other. Mindy had an apartment in Boca Raton that she bought with her inheritance. Boca Raton is a town south of Palm Beach filled with affluent, relocated, mostly Jewish Long Islanders. It doesn't really appeal to me, particularly because everyone tries so hard to have what everyone else has and look like everyone else. The houses, although affluent, all look alike. Everyone drives the same Mercedes, wears the same styles and, worst of all, has the same hairstyles.

Mindy liked Boca; she fit right in. She sat glued to her TV every day. I never realized back then that Mindy had a drinking problem. She seemed like a nice Jewish girl, a *shana maidalach*. One weekend, I stayed overnight at Mrs. Cook's house. She thought it was easier if I just stayed at her home so I didn't argue. It was a trip to be a guest in such an over the top home. I hadn't told Mindy about my clients, except that they were wealthy women from Palm Beach. I called her from Mrs. Cook's home and asked her to pick me up so we could go out for a bite to eat at a nearby restaurant. All I told her was that I was staying at the home of a client in Palm Beach. I gave her the address and directions on how to get there. After I hung up, I told the butler I was going to the back den to watch television. It was the room I knew to be the furthest in the house from the front door, the equivalent of about three city blocks. When Mindy came, the butler would have to open the huge front entrance door and walk her all the way through at least ten magnificent rooms to reach the room I was in.

I heard the doorbell ring. I pictured the butler answering the door and showing Mindy in. She got to me and just stood there with her mouth wide open. I brought her back through the house to the grand staircase. Mr. and Mrs. Cook were just leaving for the evening and coming down the stairs. Mr. Cook was dressed in a tux and Mrs. Cook in a backless, sequined pale blue evening gown, wearing some huge yellow diamonds.

"Have a nice evening, kids—drive carefully—and Byron will let you in when you come back. You'll need your rest for the ladies tomorrow."

Mindy and I got into her car. She didn't say a word, driving up A1A towards the restaurant in silence. Halfway there, she pulled over to the side of the road and started screaming, "Who the fuck was that?"

Sophia moved to Palm Beach from Beverly Hills to get away from the earthquakes in L.A. They were afraid that their massive outdoor modern art sculptures would be destroyed. I went to see her on one of my trips to Palm Beach to cut hair.. She answered the door of her penthouse at Breakers

Row One. Her two little white Maltese dogs came running up to me as if to report something horrible. Sophia had large, dark circles around her eyes and she had lost so much weight, her clothes just hung on her. We sat down on the couch and she told me what was happening in her life. "Mark, as you can see, darling, things are not quite as marvelous as the last time we saw each other."

"Sophia, are you feeling all right?"

"My marriage, darling, is in a shambles. I'm getting a divorce. My husband was having an affair with another woman. Friends heard the rumors that he was seeing Olivia DeHaviland's daughter who used to be a friend of mine; I introduced them. It was absolutely horrible. I had him followed by a private detective. While we were at the Beverly Hills Hotel, I confronted him with the evidence that my private detective had gathered and I asked him to just be truthful with me, to have the decency to admit what was going on. What a madman I'd married, darling. He began beating me with his fists, screaming that I had ruined everything. He told me I could've had anything I wanted, that he'd given me a beautiful daughter and what more could I want! A security guard had to drag him off Alexa and me. It seems the story was leaked to local TV reporters and Ted was mortified that his personal life was being paraded in the press. It's absolutely horrid. Alexa is taking it very badly. She's going to have to see a therapist. She's scared to death of her father."

She called me twice a day and talked for hours. I always thought her husband was a bit of a tyrant, but I was sorry to see it end so painfully for Sophia. She clearly loved this man who had betrayed her. I began to wonder if any men, gay or straight, were capable of being faithful, myself included. Sofia also confided that she'd been diagnosed with Multiple

Sclerosis. Even as she bared her soul to me, I couldn't bring myself to tell her that I was HIV positive. I thought she knew, because of the talk we had years ago in New York, but once she said, "You've been tested, right?" I nodded "Yes," but never said what the results were. "Good, then we don't have to worry about you."

"Sophia, I feel so badly. I wish I knew what to say to make you feel better."

"I'm really no different than anyone else, darling. Everyone is walking around with some disease. The only difference between them and me is that I know what mine is, darling."

I had now changed jobs three times and could not find a salon I was happy with. I was back working at Donsuki on Madison Avenue, but most of my income was now being generated from my Palm Beach clients and clients at home on Monday nights. I was enjoying my "traveling hairstylist" role as they wrote about me in Town & Country.

"What would it take to get you to come to Memphis?" Mrs. Price aasked.

It was hard to say 'no' to Jean Price. She was a woman who was used to getting what she wanted. She was in her sixties, with light brown hair, and she was the Grande Dame of Memphis. We modeled me and Memphis after these other hairdressers who went to Charlotte, North Carolina one weekend a month and came back with thousands of dollars. I had never been to the South, and I was a bit scared about venturing into conservative southern territory. I had a double whammy. I was gay and Jewish.

Mrs. Price made all the arrangements. We would rent a tacky old beauty parlor that was closed on Sunday and Monday and I would keep all the money I made after expenses. I couldn't believe she went so far out of her way. She wouldn't even let me give her a free haircut. I was so grateful. I booked my flight to Memphis, not knowing what to expect. It was January, the year after Sylvia died. Memphis reminded me of Syracuse, except people had more columns in front of their houses and it was warm. It was very suburban, middle America. When I first arrived, I couldn't understand what people were saying sometimes because of the accent. That accent took some time to get used to, but now I can barely hear it. I was convinced all the waiters were trying to hit on me, but they were really just being friendly. I decided beforehand that I was going to be up front and tell people right away that I was Jewish and gay. Of course, it isn't that easy to do. I mean you can't exactly say, "Hi, I'm Mark. I'm Jewish and gay. I'll be cutting your hair today." But most women start out asking a lot of personal questions, like, "Where do you go to church?" and "Are you married?" Of course, these are the best questions, because it opened up the door to tell them you are Jewish and gay. Everyone seemed pretty cool about it though, and if they felt any prejudice towards me, they hid it well, except for a few. They just didn't know many "openly" gay people.

After my first trip, the hairdressers in Memphis threatened to report me for working without a state license, so I got a Tennessee license and made arrangements to come down one Sunday and Monday per month. Sometimes I'd handle fifty-five women in two days. It was exhausting, but it was great money. We had to find another salon to rent, because the other hairdressers at the beauty parlor threatened to quit if I came back. I toured Graceland and ate ribs at Corky's. I was becoming an honorary Memphian. I think my new clients really liked me, as I did them. I wondered if when they went home, they said, "He's such a nice boy, if only he'd just find Jesus and give up that lifestyle of his." They thought I was going to Hell. But I hoped that as a result of meeting me and getting to know me, they'd think twice about voting against gay rights issues. I hoped that once they got to know me and found out that I was like them in more ways than I was different, it would be harder for them to not like gays and Jews.

One woman intrigued me right from the start. Bonnie Martin was a tall elegant brunette, and President of the Garden Club of the United States. Her hair looked like Margaret Thatcher's. The first time I cut her hair, while I was starting to blow it, she looked at me with a poker straight face and remarked, "It looks like rats have been sucking on it." Another memorable character was a ninety-three year old woman they all called GaGa. They called her GaGa because her grandchildren couldn't pronounce 'grandma'.

GaGa told me, "Ah went out and bought mahself a red Jaguar convertible for mah eightieth birthday. Ah used to drive it all over town. Then one day, Ah traded it in for a Black Mercedes Sedan. All mah family was wondering what happened to the Red Jag, but were afraid to ask. One Sunday dinner Ah figured Ah'd give 'em the explanation they were waitin' for—so Ah told them. 'Ah guess you're all wonderin' what happened to mah red Jaguar. Well, it seems like all Ah do these days is go to funerals and it just didn't seem fittin' to keep pullin' up to the cemetery in that red car, so Ah bough mahself a more appropriate vehicle.'"

I told GaGa I was admiring a ring that Pat Cook wears and I thought it was a birthstone because it was sort of yellow. When I told her what a pretty birthstone she had, she told me it was a real diamond, a canary diamond. "Oh yes, Ah have one just like it," she said.

"Why don't you wear yours? Pat Cook wears hers all the time." "Well, Ah guess she hasn't had hers quite as long as Ah've had mine."

She one day said, "Mark, Ah hope Ah die on a weekend when you come."

I was really beginning to love all my new "grand dames" from Palm Beach and Memphis. I hadn't told any of them that I was HIV positive. On top of being Jewish and gay, I didn't think they could accept that much reality. I hated having to hide this secret. In AA, we learned "you're only as sick as your secrets." But this secret was different. This one could ruin my career, and also, I didn't want everyone to treat me as if I were dying.

I'd been HIV positive for ten years. I'd never been sick in all that time. My T-cells are always the same. Everyone else I knew who had been positive as long as I had been had either developed an opportunistic infection or was dead. I decided to stop going to HIV / AA meetings. It was too depressing to constantly see and hear about people dying all the time. I didn't really worry about myself anymore. Day after day, I'd wake up alive, not the least bit sick. I thought when I was diagnosed, that I'd get sick and die. When I didn't, I figured I'd just live in the present and hope for the best. Watching my parents and friends die and facing a life-threatening illness without getting sick have given me a unique perspective on life. I know that all any of us has is Today. Tomorrow may never come. Most people know this intellectually, but until the reality hits home, you don't really feel it. I'm truly grateful every day to be alive. Maybe, if I were not HIV positive, I wouldn't enjoy life as much as I do. Today is the only day you really have. Yesterday is gone. Tomorrow is no guarantee.

EPILOGUE

Writing this book felt very cathartic. Unique experiences were happening to me and around me, but I wasn't truly there. By writing this book, I experienced things and feelings for the first time and faced what really happened and finally let it all go. My life is now beautiful and meaningful. I have had a wonderful relationship with John for ten years and we had a commitment ceremony in July. We have two beautiful homes in Miami Beach and Fire Island Pines. My career is still glamorous of sorts. I work for myself in my own salon and call my own shots. Once in awhile, a client like Mary Wells Lawrence, who is one of the nicest women in the world, will fly me to an island like Mustique or Cap Ferrer in the South of France. I still work in New York, Palm Beach, Miami and Memphis. John and Sophia threw me a fiftieth birthday party and everyone from Palm Beach and New York and Memphis were there, like Mike Cannon from Town & Country, Mrs. Don Shula, Ana Lisa Soros, Mary Wells, Vern O'Hara (HH Princess of Rajpipla), Kathy Loebb (Miss Mississippi) and Anne Miller of Memphis. So was my cousin, Mickie Rocker, who reminds me so much of Sylvia. My cousin Janene Brookner who is famous in her own right as a CIA agent, who sued the CIA (Warner Brothers bought the rights to her life story.) and won, came to the party. My birth nephew Dan, from Watertown, also came and Louis flew all the way from Buenos Aires, Argentina. It was on top of a building on 89th and Madison and overlooked Central Park, the city, the Hudson and Jersey. Everyone from my salon was there. I have never been sick one day in my life with any HIV related problems. My blood work is better than it was twenty years ago. I forget it is even an issue. Sophia also found out she does not have Multiple Sclerosis, but had mercury poisoning, which is not life threatening. John has mostly overcome his OCD and is acting in theater in Miami. It seems everyone has some kind of initials wrong with them. My life seems to be a series of complicated problems to solve. But working it through and coming out the other side has given me a great vantage point from which to view the world. The spiritual connection to your higher power comes from a series of conflicts and resolutions and if you embrace your challenges rather than avoid them, you will eventually ascend to a higher level of existence. When I go to The Pines every summer, I see the ghosts of Ralph and Carl, Dwain and all the others. How I miss them. I see the young, beautiful boys dancing the night away like no one had ever had this "religious experience" before, oblivious to the ghosts of the past that appear to me. They'll just have to find out what it's all about for themselves. But hopefully, because of people like the friends I knew who died and fought the good fight, it won't be quite as hard for them as it was for us. One summer, as I walked alongside The Pines harbor with my friend, Robin Byrd, who has a strip show on cable, we came upon a beautiful white-haired old woman, walking along the beach. Robin knew her and introduced her to me as Alice Thorp, the first and oldest resident of The Pines. "Alice, this is my

EPILOGUE

friend, Mark." "Who? Mark who?" "His name is Mark Okun." I wondered why she wanted to know my last name. She'll just forget it. "I came here in the 1930s, young man. There were no houses here then, no electricity, no anything. My husband and I came here because we were nudists. A group of us used to go to Jones Beach until they chased us off. That's when we came to The Pines. We camped out on the beach and soaked up the sun during the day. There were no houses here then and there was no one here to bother us. I can still walk to town every day at ninety-six, but someone has to take me home on a golf cart because I get too tired to walk the two miles back home." I wondered if she was tan all over. She told me that in the 30s, the Grove was already a gay town, but gay men were not allowed to own property. The straight homeowners would only rent to gay men, but not to lesbians. I thought to myself they should see it now, it's all lesbians." She continued, "I worked to make sure that this section on the east end of The Pines was designated a protected wetland. It's the cranberry bog and no one can build here." I thought of all the changes she saw over the years, from bare beach and bare ass to beach shacks and now to million-dollar, oceanfront homes. The social changes from a nudist colony to a family town to a predominantly gay community. I hope someday to walk the harbor as an old man, to be introduced to some hot young guy as the oldest living person with HIV. Will it even be important then? I'll keep alive the stories of Ralph and Carl, of Dwain and Potassa, and they'll wonder what it was like to have seen and done so much. I still miss Abe and Sylvia and all my friends who've gone before me. As much as I've tried to avoid it though, happiness and contentment seem to have found me. I used to think I would die young; now I realize it's too late!

www.ingramcontent.com/pod-product-compliance
Lightning Source LLC
Chambersburg PA
CBHW032035290426
44110CB00012B/811